PSYCHOLOGICAL THERAPIES IN PRIMARY CARE

PSYCHOLOGICAL THERAPIES IN PRIMARY CARE

Setting Up A Managed Service

Joan Foster and Antonia Murphy

KARNAC

LONDON   NEW YORK

First published in 2005 by
H. Karnac (Books) Ltd.
6 Pembroke Buildings, London NW10 6RE

British Library Cataloguing in Publication Data

A C.I.P. for this book is available from the British Library

ISBN: 1 85575 343 X

Edited, designed and produced by The Studio Publishing
Services Ltd, Exeter EX4 8JN

Printed in Great Britain

10 9 8 7 6 5 4 3 2 1

www.karnacbooks.com

Contents

About the authors

Joan Foster is Chair of the National Association of Counsellors and Psychotherapists in Primary Care (CPC). She has worked as a Primary Care Counsellor since 1992. She has also worked as a trainer in time-limited counselling and supervision, runs a number of training courses for CPC, and has been a provider of a primary care counselling service.

Joan acts as consultant to a number of PCTs in the establishment and running of primary care counselling services and is involved in interview panels and in evaluation of services.

As Chair of CPC, Joan was a member of the Department of Health Workforce Action Team, Primary Care Sub-Group, addressing workforce planning, education and training issues for adult Mental Health Services.

Her paper on 'Counselling in primary care and the new NHS' was published in 2000 in the *British Journal of Guidance and Counselling*, *28*(2), and she is joint author of *Quality in Counselling in Primary Care. A Guide for Effective Commissioning and Clinical Governance*.

Antonia Murphy is a graduate in Psychodynamic Counselling from the WPF. Following a move to Nottingham in 1993, she worked as a counsellor in primary care and subsequently as Co-ordinator of the Southern Derbyshire Health Authority managed counselling service from 1995–2002. This latter role was invaluable in extending her experience and awareness of the complexities of the role of the therapist in the setting of general practice.

Over the past few years Antonia has become involved in the national delivery of counselling and psychotherapy in primary care through both the Network of Service Providers and the National Forum for Training Standards. She is Vice Chair of the Association of Counsellors and Psychotherapists in Primary Care (CPC).

Antonia is the author of several papers on aspects of psychotherapeutic practice in primary care and the NHS. She is the former editor of the *Journal for the Foundation of Psychotherapy and Counselling* and currently an editorial board member of the *Journal of Psychodynamic Practice* and Editor of *CPC Review*.

She currently works in private practice as a counsellor, supervisor and trainer, and continues her work with CPC.

Foreword

I am delighted to write the foreword to this book. I have watched the rapid development of primary care counselling since the introduction of primary care commissioning in 1999 and the NHS Alliance has recognized its importance, not only clinically but also structurally.

We know the case for the effectiveness of primary care counselling is now well made, and its inclusion as a treatment of choice in the NICE Guidelines for Treatment of Depression is a recognition of that fact. However, good quality counselling needs more than good practitioners. In today's NHS it needs co-ordination and management, linking in with other services and to be accountable. This book tells the reader how to achieve just that.

Written in an easy, accessible style, it addresses the nuts and bolts as well as the strategic issues that need to be dealt with by every primary care counselling service manager in the country. It also acts as a bridge between two worlds – the medical model and the holistic counselling model. Indeed, counselling also builds a bridge to the psychiatric approach to working with patients with mental health problems.

The process of change in the NHS, and particularly in primary care, has been extremely rapid over the past few years, and the NHS Alliance has worked to assist primary care colleagues through what has sometimes seemed a morass. This pace of change continues, and this book will greatly assist all those involved in delivering psychological therapies services in primary care, now and in the future. It is essential and timely reading for managers, commissioners, and practitioners.

Joan Foster and Antonia Murphy are national leads in this area and have brought their wide experience together to produce this book.

Dr Michael Dixon
Chair NHS Alliance

Introduction

About this book

Since you have picked up this book something about the title must be of interest to you. Perhaps you are a new counselling service manager working in the National Health Service (NHS) or maybe a commissioning manager seeking to consolidate the provision of psychological therapies in primary care? Or maybe you're an experienced counsellor who has been around the block a few times, come up against problems, and could do with a new view on things? Whatever your interest or inclination we hope that you'll find much of what follows to be informative, essential, and accessible in the context of providing fully professional, effective, and efficient counselling and psychological therapy services for today's NHS.

We have written the book with the following readership in mind and trust that it will be a useful guide to:

- Commissioners and providers of NHS counselling and psychological therapy services;
- PCT chief executives and directors;
- PCT mental health leads;

- Mental Health Trust directors and managers;
- Individual counselling and psychotherapy clinicians;
- Other providers of counselling services such as private providers, voluntary sector organisations and related professionals.

The content of the book relates to the effective organization and management of counselling services – a clinical service. The context for the book is the NHS, and in particular 'primary care'. This means work taking place in GP surgeries. However, many of the issues and problems we tackle in the following chapters will be typical of other organizational settings. Thus, we would expect the book to have a wider readership than just those working within the NHS.

Using this book

We intend this to be a 'How To' book. It is written, we hope, in small, easy to access sections with lots of practical guidance, descriptive examples, and tips gained from our own and others' experience. The first chapter sets out to describe and elaborate on the case for a managed service. Chapters Two, Three, Four and Five cover all aspects of the design and components of a managed service – the meat in the sandwich. Particular reference is given to the clinical implications for counselling practitioners in Chapters Five and Six. Training issues are covered in Chapter Six for manager, counsellor, and supervisor. The final chapter considers the impact and influence of counselling and psychological therapy in the NHS.

We hope that our combined knowledge and experience of the intricacies and complexities of the field will help you manage the challenges of providing the best possible counselling provision to patients in today's NHS.

At present, the validity of a systematic approach to the management and provision of counselling is still hotly debated within the profession. Meanwhile, the validity of having any sort of counselling provision, managed or otherwise, is still debated within the NHS. There are differences around the definitions of psychological therapy and where counselling 'fits' in NHS approaches to the treatment of mental illness.

The authors have worked in the field of NHS counselling for over fifteen years apiece, both as counsellors, supervisors, trainers, and managers. We have written this book from real practice and experience, both clinical and managerial. We also draw extensively from our work over recent years as chair and vice chair of the Association of Counsellors and Psychotherapists in Primary Care (CPC).

We recognize the inherent difficulty of working as counselling clinicians within an organizational context, when the internal therapeutic alliance needs to be preserved. We also recognize and acknowledge the real funding and operational constraints of the NHS. But with a professional and personal knowledge of effectiveness of therapeutic work we feel it is better for good psychological therapy to be available in the mainstream of health provision than isolated and weakened on the outside. We would not argue that establishing a managed service means all will be well, but rather it is a frame within which due care can be taken of patients. That there is a now a real need for this book is an indication of the scale of high-quality counselling services already established in today's NHS. However, we are also aware of the size of the task ahead in order that the expansion of effective, managed provision is the norm rather than the exception. It is to be hoped that the growth of primary care psychological therapies will be a welcome addition to the resources of the NHS and that the place of the primary care counsellor will be firmly established and valued in the NHS through the secure framework of the managed service, good terms and conditions of employment for counsellors, and safe effective practice for patients.

Using the book

To help you navigate your way around we have used a combination of information, direct experience, and case material to emphasize the content. In the more practical chapters you will find authors' tips, which are drawn from actual examples in the field. We have also created some characters to represent the different roles within particular areas of the NHS. These characters appear in role at various junctures in the text to help establish different ideas at different times. We intend that this should help the reader to understand the varying points of view that can often cause difficulty. It is also our aim to make the book an easy and enjoyable read.

Terminology

The term psychological therapy is used to describe therapeutic treatments where a professional therapist – counsellor, psychotherapist, or counselling psychologist –

provides a series of sessions to a patient in order to discuss their problems, develop solutions, or work through an understanding of their pain and illness. This may well be a rather specialist understanding compared with more general descriptions of psychological therapy services, which may also include self-help interventions, guided reading, advice, support, etc. For the most part we have used the terms counsellor, psychotherapist, and psychological therapist interchangeably.

CHAPTER ONE

WHY A MANAGED COUNSELLING SERVICE?

Outline and aims

This chapter explains the background to the development of counselling in primary care and the managed counselling service. It outlines the main structural changes in the National Health Service (NHS) in recent years and their impact on the evolution of counselling provision. It also explores the nature of counselling services in relation to current and future mental health strategy and policy, and to integrated psychological therapy services.

* * * * *

Looking around

Counselling has emerged during the last decade as a distinct profession in the health service. As a clinical service in the NHS it has undergone rapid growth in the last few years. While there is still continued debate among providers, purchasers, and planners as to the place and credibility of counselling within the NHS, there is now considerable support, investment, and commitment to its provision both in primary care and in the wider NHS. In fact, the increased level of debate as to its validity, its place, its function is a measure of the seriousness with which counselling in primary care is now taken. A growing research evidence base now supports the clinical and cost effectiveness of counselling.

While some arguments are still heard concerning the inclusion of counselling and the psychological therapies within the province of national health care, these tend to be arguments as to the appropriateness of the setting for such treatment approaches rather than arguments about their clinical validity.

There is, in fact, now widespread agreement and well-established evidence for the place of psychological therapies in NHS mental health care. Service users rate access to psychological therapy as crucial. Not only that, but the recent Department of Health (DoH) report *Organising and Delivering Psychological Therapies* (DoH, 2004) states quite unequivocally that

> Psychological therapies should no longer be regarded as optional. Nor should access to effective psychological therapies be constrained by the vagaries of local geography and history ... psychological therapies are fundamental to basic mental health care and can make a highly significant contribution to outcome and user satisfaction.

This is now the official line and the backdrop against which local services can be managed and delivered. The key words here are that services should not be constrained by local history/geography – in other words by previous poor practice, lack of trained clinical staff, personalities, prejudices, and lack of knowledge. There are many different ways of delivering effective psychological therapies and a great number of different professionals are involved:

counsellors, psychotherapists, psychologists, and mental health workers. This lack of a one-way approach offers genuine flexibility and the opportunity for patients to receive good psychological care that fits their needs. But it is also sometimes a recipe for muddle, confusion, paralysis, and professional rivalry.

Evolution – making the fit

So, rather than examine the case for counselling within the NHS, this book starts from the premise that counselling services have a serious and necessary place in the spectrum of psychological therapy provision. Consequently, it is necessary to be serious and professional about how such services should best be delivered. It is also necessary to be informed about the nature of the different psychological therapies in order that service users (patients) can achieve better choice and better engagement with treatment in the NHS. However, in many areas access to counselling and/or other psychological therapies is confusing and patchy. In order to improve this and to provide the most effective treatment, it is essential that clear leadership and management of counselling within the overall framework of psychological therapy services is provided and adequately resourced.

Over recent years there has been a flurry, rather than an avalanche, of debate around the notion of the management of counselling and psychological therapy services in the NHS within the profession itself. For many front-line counsellors it is hard enough to be effective clinicians in the face of major structural changes in the NHS without worrying about who is managing what and why. For others, management is not an attractive option – many counsellors entered the profession to work as clinicians after previous long-running careers in management. But the issue of management becomes important once services are up and running and resources are limited and competed for. It also becomes necessary when clear relationships within the overall structure of a mental health or primary care trust (PCT) are required to avoid interprofessional rivalries interfering with access to appropriate treatment. Once a management structure is in place, the service has a voice and becomes accountable. Clinical governance requirements of good practice can be demonstrated, outcomes can be evaluated, and the service can be measured as to whether it delivers value for money.

Individually, as a counsellor, you may prefer to stay out of the tussle for power and resources between various interested and competing parties. You may want to remain unaffected by such matters – you may be frightened of entering the fray. But if you enter the jungle you need to learn to live and survive with the other animals! In a new environment, where resources are limited, adaptation is necessary for survival and evolution. But you also need to be able to preserve your species identity because you have something different and unique to offer. One of the most interesting and delicate tensions around working as a counselling therapist in the NHS is that between fitting in, being useful, and being different.

Primary care rules, OK?

Recent changes in the NHS might lead us to believe that we now have an NHS that is led much more by clinical staff and their priorities for patients. This rhetoric is particularly strong in relation to the changes in the organization of primary care. However, in his address to the Fourth Annual Healthcare Conference in November 2003, Dr Michael Dixon of the NHS Alliance (*CPC Review*, 2004) warned that

> The NHS is controlled by a chain of management from the chief exec in Whitehall, to the SHA chief execs and down to the chief exec of each PCT. We have created a managerialised NHS that effectively excludes the voices of front-line clinicians and lay people.

If Michael Dixon is right – and recent experience over mental health policy certainly bears out his opinion – this is the time for front-line staff in primary care to build on the strength of their relationships with each other and with their patients so that work in primary care becomes the new authority in the NHS. Counselling services are an important part of this barefoot approach and are already proving influential in improving the lives of patients. The basis of this book is that the patchwork of counselling provision that emerged over the past twenty years is ripe for consolidation through organization in order that therapeutic work with individual patients will be strengthened rather than eroded. We are not in any sense advocating a crude management model for purposes of control, target setting, and bean counting, but rather a service-orientated approach to the provision of specialist psychological therapy managed by clinicians who really know the nature of the therapeutic endeavour and who can build good working relationships with others.

Counselling is not an approach to health that takes place quickly or simply – it is hard, complex work and very often doesn't fix things in an obvious or even ostensibly positive way. Counselling helps people face their pain and tolerate frustration. Good counselling service management needs to be designed with the same aims in mind.

Background

Historically, counsellors first started working in primary general practice in the late 1960s. By 1992, 31% of English and Welsh practices reported having a counsellor on site (Mellor-Clark, Simms-Ellis, & Burton, 2001; Sibbald, Addington-Hall, Brenneman, & Freeling, 1993). The first reference to 'practice counsellors' was made in 1975 (Marsh & Barr, 1975), describing marriage guidance counselling in a group practice. The emergence of practice counsellors at this time reflected a developing awareness of psychosocial factors in individual well-being and a new way of thinking about patients in the medical context. It is important here to acknowledge the work of Michael and Enid Balint in the 1960s. They focused on the patient and on exploring an emotional understanding of their work as general practitioners (GPs) in the NHS. The resulting 'Balint Groups' became a forum for GPs to explore their own anxieties and difficulties in their work. Many GPs who participated began to incorporate a more holistic approach to their work and were able to challenge the defences used by many practitioners to protect themselves from the pain they dealt with day by day. This provided fertile ground for the introduction of psychotherapeutic thinking and interventions within primary care.

Service development

Initially, in the 1970s and 1980s, we saw a somewhat haphazard introduction of counselling provision into the NHS. Most of the counsellors employed had taken up counselling as a second career, having come from professions as wide and as varied as teaching, accountancy, building, social work, and marriage. Many of these counsellors were pioneers, the first counsellor in their surgery, having worked in either the voluntary or the private sector. They were self-employed, and often isolated within the primary health care team. They were often recruited by enlightened GPs to some extent familiar with the paradigm of counselling or psychotherapy.

Traditionally the growth of primary care counselling has been on an individual basis. It is estimated that in 1999, 60% of counsellors were self-employed, 30% were employed and 10% were volunteers or students. Many of those holding self-employed contracts were in fundholding GP surgeries, which were encouraged to 'go it alone' – they held their own budgets and could, to a certain extent, decide how to allocate their funds for various services. The self-employed counsellor found a place in those practices that were more 'psychologically minded' and could see the need for a primary care counsellor as part of the team. In addition there were other motivations – many GPs employed practice counsellors as an attempt to avoid the long waiting lists for clinical psychology, psychiatry, and psychotherapy at the secondary level and to lower costs. However, this revealed some confusion as to the differences between the various psychological therapies and misunderstanding as to the process and outcome of therapeutic work. Much of this original confusion still permeates thinking today and causes problems for the design of effective mental health services both in primary and secondary care.

The vast majority of these newly recruited counsellors were trained to offer 'open-ended' counselling and many struggled to adapt to limitations later imposed upon them, such as that of time-limited work. Other aspects of work within the primary care frame also caused difficulty; for example, the interface between confidentiality and collaboration. Counsellors had to learn how to discuss their work in this new context while maintaining the safety of the counselling frame. Many aspects of a hitherto one-to-one alliance between counsellor and patient were now deeply affected by the context. Decisions were made by non-clinicians driven by issues of funding and also, possibly, of control.

From these early beginnings it became clear that working in the NHS was a whole new ball-game for counsellors. They needed to work as part of a team in a large organization – to collaborate, to provide feedback, to refer on, to take part in clinical discussions, to develop protocols, to manage and plan service development, etc. They were now accountable not just to their patients but to their funders, and needed to be able to provide counselling that complemented existing services within the NHS. The professional primary care counsellor had arrived.

The profession has legs!

Not surprisingly, with the emerging professionalism of the individual counsellor in the NHS came organization to accompany and hasten the development. In the late 1980s Dr Graham Curtis-Jenkins formed the charitable foundation, The Counselling in Primary Care Trust and led, in the early 1990s, the clarion cry for professionalism, specialist training, standards and resources, etc., for counsellors working in primary care. From these early origins sprang the National Network of Providers of NHS Primary Care Counselling, active today as a forty-strong forum for discussion and lobbying solely comprising counselling service managers.

Notably, the Counselling in Primary Care Trust also spawned the formation of the first professional body to set standards for membership and to represent professional counsellors and psychotherapists in the NHS: the Association of Counsellors and Psychotherapists in Primary Care (CPC). CPC was created in 1998 and has been growing in membership and in authority ever since. At the same time the Faculty for Health Care Practitioners (formerly Counsellors in Medical Settings), a division of the British Association of Counselling and Psychotherapy (BACP), has been influential for over twenty years in providing guidance and advice in the arena of counselling in medical settings. The United Kingdom Council for Psychotherapy has also recently introduced a new section for Psychotherapeutic Counsellors, which could include counsellors trained to the CPC's designated standard for primary care counsellors. Finally, we have seen cooperation between these various bodies under the auspices of the Counselling and Psychotherapy Training Forum for Primary Care in terms of standard setting, training, and selection, in readiness for future regulation. If the proliferation of organizations is anything to go by, the counselling profession in the NHS has definitely got legs – it is virtually a centipede!

Changing times

As counselling in primary care emerged in this *ad hoc* way there was a parallel recognition of the enormous number of patients presenting with mental health problems in primary care. In 1999 The National Service Framework for Mental Health in England stated: 'Generally, for every one hundred individuals that consult their GP with a mental health problem, nine will be referred to specialist services for assessment and advice, or for treatment.' (DoH, 1999)

This invites the question as to what was happening to the other ninety-one out of every hundred for whom primary care teams remained responsible! At the same time the lion's share of resources (money) was spent on specialist mental health services – so things didn't quite add up. Regardless of the statistical truths, few disagreed that primary care had long managed and cared for the vast majority of people with mental health problems. Admittedly, many of these problems and aspects of illness were hidden within complex social and somatic presentations and were often either avoided or overlooked.

As this new focus was being developed, the role of the GP as a single-handed practitioner who could work holistically with the patient was being replaced by group practices with a more organized approach to service provision. In addition, families were now being viewed from a systemic approach and the possibility of working with the 'whole' person was becoming more difficult. Thus, the period in which primary care counselling undertook its most dramatic growth – the 1990s – was also one of significant change within the NHS and within thinking about mental health. These changes were further compounded by the abolition of fund-holding in 1999 and the introduction of primary care commissioning. This development led to a totally different way of managing and commissioning services for primary care in England and, subsequently, in Wales, Scotland and Northern Ireland. From 1 April 1999 every GP or group practice became part of a Primary Care Group (PCG).

A PCG usually served a population of about 100,000, and all the GP surgeries within the PCG had to work together with a PCG Board, Chief Executive, and Staff. The government thinking was to abolish postcode prescribing and ensure equity of provision across the whole of the PCG. By 1 April 2003, all PCGs had become Primary Care Trusts (PCTs) – 481 PCGs replaced by 302 PCTs. A Primary Care Trust is a legal body and is able to employ staff.

What was happening to the primary care counsellor during this period of enormous change? In a nutshell, their world changed totally. The day of the independent self-employed counsellor working in their own surgery, with their private supervisor, was over. The reasons: clinical governance and equity of access – two of the main planks of reform in the government's NHS Plan published in 1998.

Following this radical re-framing of primary care, health services were now being driven by primary care commissioning from within the primary care organizations. Clinical governance was the new mission, central to the government's reforms. This spelt out that all services were to be delivered within standards set via professional self-regulation thus:

> Clinical governance and life long learning will help instil quality at a local level throughout commissioning. This

places services such as counselling hitherto at the mercy of individual innovative practices or Trusts much more centre stage and much more under scrutiny. The government's National Institute of Clinical Excellence (NICE) will be instrumental in ensuring the NHS. Both are founded on the principle that health professionals must be responsible and accountable for their own practice. [DoH, 2000, para. 3.43]

Clinical governance will provide:

. . . a framework through which NHS organisations are accountable for continuously improving the quality of their services and safeguarding high standards of care by creating an environment in which excellence in clinical care will flourish. [Donaldson, 1998]

Admittedly, such initiatives raised as many questions as they answered but none the less the arrival of Primary Care Trusts meant that the employment of counsellors in the haphazard and sometimes exploitative and unethical forms of old could not continue. Under the newly constituted primary care organizations, counselling in primary care had to meet the standards of clinical governance. Professional NHS counselling now needed its own coherent, distinct clinical organization and management to match the organization and structure of the NHS. Such changes made it necessary for those of us working in the field of professional counselling in the NHS to set and maintain standards of excellence in order that good quality, well managed counselling can be offered through every PCT in the country.

More questions than answers

In PCTs where primary care counselling was already provided in some form, questions were now asked about the effectiveness, quality, delivery, equity, and cost, etc., of such services. In PCTs where there was no such service, or rudimentary provision only, questions were being asked as to whether and how primary care counselling would be delivered.

Alongside the clinical governance guidelines the similarly ubiquitous notion of equity of access appeared in the same NHS plan and raised the stakes even higher for service provision and commissioning decisions.

'Equity of access' meant that if one practice offered a service in the PCG/T then they all had to. At about this time there were counsellors in 51% of GP surgeries. This created an interesting dilemma for those Primary Care Trusts who were prepared, or aware enough, to face the problem. How do you spread 51% over 100% without either reducing services or putting in more money?

What added to the difficulty facing primary care counselling services was that very few in the counselling world recognized this as an issue, and even fewer in the then new PCGs. This was in part because, as far as the NHS was concerned, counsellors did not exist! Despite constant expansion and considerable clinical evidence of effectiveness there was no recognized pay spine for counsellors within the NHS.

At the time of writing the DoH is introducing 'Agenda for Change', which will analyse all professions working in the NHS and allocate them to a pay spine. Job profiles for counsellors have been evaluated and approved and allocated to three pay bands – bands 5 to 7 (Appendix 1).

Job profiles for the counselling manager and counsellor consultant are being evaluated. This is an enormous step forward in robustly establishing the profession in the NHS at last.

The emergence of the managed counselling service

In 2000/2001 The National Primary Care Research and Development Centre Tracker Survey of Primary Care Groups and Trusts demonstrated the following:

PCG/PCT provision of primary care counselling services:

73.6%	Continue existing provision and/or move to a PCG/T wide service
12.5%	Under discussion
2.8%	Not on agenda/no agreed policy
6.9%	No primary care counselling provision
4.2%	Missing data.

At this point, then, it seemed that the creation of the Primary Care Organizations (PCOs) had galvanized much of the existing counselling provision into organizing itself in relation to the NHS changes. To survive and thrive organization was required. In large parts of the country primary care counselling had established itself with enough clinical integrity and effectiveness in the independent/fund-holding GP practices of old prior to the creation of the PCOs to be able to move ahead as an integral part of NHS mental health service provision and planning. Expansion had taken place in many areas, so that by the time the PCOs were set up counselling services in over 70% of the country had some form of primary care counselling on a PCG/T-wide basis. In other areas, however, funding was spread more thinly. In others still, existing individual counsellors were sacked and 'alternative' provision drawn up from within Mental Health Trusts/primary care teams.

Thus, a very inconsistent national picture in relation to NHS counselling provision emerged from this period of dramatic change, and persists to date. Despite the growing awareness of the clinical effectiveness of counselling, the availability of an evidence base, the improvement in training and the setting of qualification standards, improved management planning and widespread patient preference and the clinical support of the majority of GPs, we cannot yet assume that all patients will have access to counselling through their GP. There are still many parts of the country where there are gaps between local needs and the services currently provided.

In a recent edition of *Improving Quality in Primary Care: A Practical Guide to the National Service Framework for Mental Health* (DoH, 2003) it is suggested that there are two main issues to consider when choosing psychological therapies:

- evidence of effectiveness;
- patient preference.

The DoH in its own evidence-based clinical practice guideline: *Treatment Choice in Psychological Therapies and Counselling* (DoH, 2001) states that: 'Psychological therapy should be routinely considered as a treatment option when assessing mental health problems' (p. 34). However, for this to be the case, professional counselling services, which now have a proven clinical evidence base, do need to be available throughout the whole of the NHS in order that patients can exercise just such a preference. In so doing they have a far greater chance of significant clinical change.

We now hear much more about integrated psychological therapy services. The idea for such a model is that this covers the whole range of different therapeutic models and professionals available in the NHS – psychodynamic to integrative counselling, psychoanalytic psychotherapy, cognitive–behavioural psychotherapy and family and systemic approaches, etc. – the whole kit and caboodle! Under such a model counselling provision can either be managed as a separate professional arm in parallel to the other mental health professionals or as an integrated part of an overall psychological therapy team.

The DoH's publication *Organising and Delivering Psychological Therapies* (2004) argues that:

> Psychological therapy provision is a multi-professional and multi-agency endeavour. Psychiatrists, psychotherapists, psychologists, counsellors, nurses, social workers and many other groups are involved all of whom need to communicate and co-ordinate effectively with one another.

It goes on to say '. . . Psychological therapies are fundamental to basic mental health care and can make a highly significant contribution to outcome and user satisfaction . . .' Its recommendations are based on a range of well-established scientific evidence but also on the professional consensus and the views of service users.

The document makes continued reference to the inclusion of counselling alongside psychology, community psychiatric nurses (CPNs) and other mental health workers as part of an integrated team of therapists able to offer an array of types of therapy to suit the patient's need and clinical assessment. However, there is an implication, not explicit, that counselling comes in under the psychology umbrella. This does not necessarily follow. Psychology and counselling are different professions. Counselling service managers can equally lead the provision of integrated psychological therapy services in primary care or remain a parallel arm.

The DoH document is an important one and contains very sensible recommendations for the integration of services, including that the co-ordination of the differing arms of psychological therapy delivery is best done: 'through a Psychological Therapies Management Committee (PTMC) in which inter-professional rivalries can be mitigated and where there is clear relationship to the overall management structure of a Trust'. Wise words indeed, and we have yet to see how such sound advice will translate itself in practice throughout the country. The use of the mnemonic PTMC bodes well for the take-up of this model. Many elements, most importantly the strength of existing relationships and the level of trust between the professions involved, will determine its success. It behoves counselling services to get their act together if they wish to remain or become a significant element of such PTMCs.

One of the main characteristics of a managed counselling service is that it can be proactive in helping the PCT to conduct health needs assessments and implement the changes to services required as a result. In other words, if counselling is in the system it can be effective both clinically and organizationally. However, paradoxically, if there is no counselling service, nor even the embryonic conditions for such, there is often an absence of knowledge and influence at the strategic level about the basic principles of therapy – no one pops up at the next Professional Executive Committee (PEC) meeting to raise the subject, no one gets to comment on the overly medicalized depression protocols produced by the local working party, etc. So, in the very places where it is most needed, the case for consolidated provision of psychological therapy often continues to be overlooked.

Primary care and mental health

Other aspects of the government's NHS plan have affected the development of counselling services beyond issues simply of management. The emphasis on clinical governance and clinical effectiveness has meant that where counselling services have flourished this has been largely due to the successful transition to a managed service that can provide accountability, team working, pathways and protocols for referral and assessment, and realistic economies of scale, as well as good terms and conditions for counsellors.

This has meant a change from the more traditional ethos of counsellors as individual practitioners to a much more complex structure in which counsellors are employed like any other health professional, with the usual pros and cons. Where once the likelihood of being offered a referral to a counsellor was based on the throw of the dice with respect to the sympathies of the individual GP and the random availability of a counsellor, a managed service provides the possibility of counselling being available to every adult patient within known protocols and guidelines of service.

The National Service Framework for Mental Health (DoH, 1999) set out many aims and challenges for NHS providers of mental health services. It was surprisingly explicit that the majority of mental health problems are best dealt with in primary care. However, counselling services have still to some extent sat uneasily within this strategy, despite being an extremely useful plank in helping PCTs meet the challenges of the government's aims in relation to improving mental health provision. We will look at why this might be so in more detail in Chapter Seven – it is, we think, a complicated tangle of various tensions – but for now it might be worth emphasizing that the very possibility, let alone the effectiveness, of counselling and psychotherapy depends totally on the patient and therapist forming and developing an effective working relationship – what is known in the trade as a therapeutic alliance. This is wholly different from deciding what is going to fix things according to a diagnosis linked to a schematic protocol. Hence, when it comes to devising mental health strategy, the paradigm of the psychological relationship rarely, if ever, drives the strategy. This is a great shame and results in much misunderstanding, unrealistic policy, and sometimes dubious treatment.

If we look more closely at the initiatives that have come out of the National Service Framework for Mental Health in relation to primary care, they have been concerned with:

- improving identification of mental health needs;
- undertaking proper assessment of mental health;
- providing effective treatments;
- organizing training for primary care staff on mental health awareness and early triage;

- developing PCT-wide protocols and guidelines on the major areas of mental health, e.g., depression, anxiety, schizophrenia, drug and alcohol misuse, and eating disorders.

Interestingly, it could be argued that all of the above could be improved by existing primary care services within which primary care counselling forms a crucial plank. But alas, government thinking appears to be driven by models of care and treatment based on secondary and psychiatric approaches to mental illness and treatment. In this vein the NHS Plan also stated that by 2004

> One thousand new graduate primary care mental health workers, trained in brief therapy techniques of proven effectiveness, will have been employed to help GPs manage and treat common mental health problems in all age groups including children. [DoH, 2000]

These are laudable aims and initiatives, but many PCTs have understandably become confused. The 'invention' of the graduate mental health workers has had the downside of encouraging PCTs to bypass the services of highly effective counsellors and psychotherapists, which many PCTs already have in place in primary care, and who could be even more useful and effective in all of the areas outlined above. At present, the graduate mental health workers are untried and untested practitioners fast-tracked through a whistle-stop training that as yet has no proven clinical evidence base. While such workers may well be a valuable addition to the primary care team they might equally be of very restricted use given their limited training and experience. They will inevitably be dependent on the skill and experience of fully trained psychological therapists and mental health practitioners in order to ensure that risk assessment and therapeutic assessments are carried out. They will need a great deal of help to be able to offer even supportive work to those patients with problems of the sort of complexity with which primary care is so familiar.

The future – integrated services?

With this background in mind, the shape of things to come in primary care may well be to move to more integrated primary care mental health teams within which the new mental health workers can integrate with specialist primary care counsellors, CPNs, and liaise with psychiatry. This may well be a very good thing all round. The management of such teams could develop from the structure of existing managed counselling services and/or psychology services. Such teams could be self-contained, responsive to and responsible for all that is required in primary care mental health such as:

- identifying and assessing a range of mental health problems and illness from the mild to the severe, from the single focused to the complex;
- co-ordinating and collaborating across specialisms and treatment options so that patients with mental health needs get what they need when they need it as well as different things at different times from different people;
- developing capacity in relation to the treatment of mental health problems among the primary care workforce through training and continued professional development;

- By and large eradicating the primary care and secondary care interface – it's not a very useful one these days;
- linking in with non-statutory agencies and organizations that can provide a wealth of options for patients.

Such developments are already in place in parts of the country with evident success.

Interestingly, models for the management of such integrated teams can be drawn from the existing managed counselling service models outlined throughout this book. Today's NHS managed counselling services already take many forms, depending on local variations in NHS Trust structures and local imperatives for the future. Due to the haphazard development of NHS counselling outlined above, managed counselling services have emerged in many shapes and sizes within a variety of trust structures – Mental Health Trusts, Community Trusts, Integrated Trusts, and Primary Care Trusts. Often within secondary trusts counselling falls under the remit of the psychology service, or mental health services. Counsellors are employed within these services on terms and conditions that are similar to those of clinical psychologists, CPNs, or other health professionals, and are managed within similar structures. In contrast, some managed services have formed directly from individual primary care practices and have been designed within primary care trusts themselves.

So, we can see from the many variations in the organizational setting for a managed counselling service that no particular model emerges as the front-runner. The questions facing each variation will be different (depending on what is now the case) and the same (depending on what should be the case). It is essential to consider the core ingredients for best practice and good organization and then apply them to your local model and needs. It is hoped that the following chapters will provide you with the basic principles of sound managed practice and a range of solutions that will further the integration of counselling within the overall panoply of psychological therapy provision.

CHAPTER TWO

BACK TO BASICS

Outline and aims

This chapter considers the necessary conditions for a managed counselling and psychological therapy service in the NHS. It outlines the main components of a managed service, looking at both the benefits and disadvantages of such from an organizational and a clinical perspective with particular relevance to the counselling clinician.

* * * * *

When considering the best conditions for a managed counselling service, the classic line 'If that's where you are going, I wouldn't start from here!' springs to mind. This is the main problem facing many primary care commissioning managers around the country. It is always infinitely more difficult changing a structure than establishing a new one, and when one recalls that a description of managing counsellors (made by a counsellor) is 'It's like herding cats!' we can see why help may be needed. In this chapter and throughout the rest of the book we are going to use a fairly typical PCT that is not based on anywhere in particular, but is generally representative, to elaborate on all the many and complex variables that need to be faced and financed (see p. 26).

Central Anywhere PCT

- 125,000 patients
- 25 practices
- Current primary care counselling provision in nineteen practices
- Thirteen practices (most were fund-holders) have counselling provided by eleven independent self-employed counsellors (two counsellors worked in two practices). The counsellors' pay varied from £15–£30 an hour. Four of them received an additional payment for administration and attendance at practice meetings. Three others received payment for their supervision costs. One was being charged room rental. The practices were very happy with the service they got from the counsellors and reluctant to change anything.
- Four practices have counselling provided by two counselling psychologists and two cognitive behaviour therapists employed by the psychology department of the local Mental Health Trust
- Four practices have counselling provided by a local voluntary counselling service
- Of the four remaining practices, two are very keen to have a counsellor, but no funding is available; one is a single-hander and had no room at all; the final practice has never made any response on the subject.
- Five of the thirteen practices that have counselling already are also Personal Medical Services (PMS) practices. The rest are General Medical Services (GMS). This will mean a different process for spending a budget allocation for counselling. For the purpose of this book, we will be assuming that the PMS practices will wish to be part of a managed counselling service.

Getting to grips

Let us imagine that, knowing they had inherited a rather mixed bag of counselling provision, the PCT had commissioned a review of the counselling provision by an external consultant. The PCT had previously agreed that it wished to have an equitable service, with equal pay and conditions for the counsellors. It wanted a clear structure with agreed protocols across the service. The PCT had not decided what was the best structure for a managed service and looked to the consultant, in consultation with all interested parties, to recommend a preferred option.

This review had identified major gaps in standards of service, pay, conditions, equity of access, accountability, referral protocols, and outcome evidence. The consultant had analysed the allocated budget to counselling in practices, the actual spend, and the hours per 1000 of the patient population that each practice was funded for. To achieve equity, the PCT was faced with the choice of a redistribution of funding, which would mean some practices were winners but some were losers, or increasing the funding.

The following key issues were identified in the review:

- lack of equity of counselling;
- lack of equitable pay and conditions for the counsellors;
- clinical governance – it was not known if the counsellors met professional standards;
- accountability – who is managing the counsellors? To whom are they accountable?;
- referral pathways were unclear;
- there were poor (if any) links with mental health colleagues in secondary care;

- audit and evaluation – none in place;
- supervision – the PCT did not know who were the supervisors of the counsellors or whether they were appropriate. There were no agreed standards for how much supervision should be provided, or how much each counsellor was receiving;
- waiting list management – there were long waiting lists in some practices;
- there was no information about cancellations or DNAs (did not attend);
- there was no data collection as to the number of patients seen;
- there was no information on presenting problems;
- there was no information on age/gender/ethnicity of patients;
- there was no information as to number of sessions per patient;
- there was no involvement in planning of mental health strategy by anyone from the counselling service;
- there was no safety policy in place for the counsellors in terms of appropriate rooms, panic buttons, etc.
- there was no policy concerning notes and record-keeping (some counsellors were keeping their clients' notes at home);
- there were no policies for retention and destruction of notes;
- there were no policies for what data should be entered on a patient's medical notes.

In addition, the consultant made the PCT aware that Inland Revenue guidance concerning what comprised self-employment or employment indicated that a counsellor working for a fixed rate of pay, for fixed hours each week would be regarded as employed. This could put the PCT at risk if the self-employed contracts were continued, as the PCT could be liable to a fine and payment of back tax.

The primary care commissioning manager who had commissioned the service review felt a bit depressed when she read the consultant's report!

Onwards and upwards!

She soon recovered, however, and used the report as a catalyst to move urgently to a managed, employed service; then there was disagreement as to where the management should be located. The choices identified were:

(a) a PCT-based service, with a counselling service manager and the counsellors employed by the PCT;
(b) a Mental Health Trust-based service, with a counselling service manager and the counsellors employed by the Mental Health Trust;
(c) a private provider, with a service manager and the counsellors employed by the private provider;
(d) a service, co-ordinated by a professional lead employed by the PCT but with counsellors employed by individual GP practices.

Option (d) had not been a choice up to late 2004, but with the move to practice-led commissioning this became an option to be considered.

The mental health lead for the PCT was a GP. He was closely involved with the review and supported the move to a managed service. However, he had concerns as to the reactions of his GP colleagues. He knew that some had very little interest in mental health issues; others were very pro counselling but equally very resistant to change and wanted things to stay as they were.

The consultant presented the report to the PEC and there was considerable debate as to the preferred option. Nationally the PCT were aware that the statistics for where the management resided were approximately as follows:

PCT:	40%
Mental Health Trust:	40%
Private/other provider:	10%
No managed service:	10%

The PCT were aware that today's NHS managed counselling service will take many forms, depending on local variations in NHS Trust structures and local imperatives for the future. Due to the haphazard development of NHS counselling as outlined in Chapter One, managed counselling services have emerged in all sorts of forms within trusts of varying types: Mental Health Trusts, Community Trusts, Integrated Trusts, and, since their formation, Primary Care Trusts. The employment terms and conditions of the counsellors as well as their clinical requirements has varied according to the overall management structure. Within mental health or secondary trusts counselling has often fallen within the remit of the psychology service or community mental health teams. Counsellors have been employed within these services on various terms and conditions similar to CPNs or other health professionals, or even on administration and clerical grades!

Competing interests

The PCT had had a lot of pressure from the local voluntary agency that provided counselling in four practices.
The agency wanted the entire contract to provide primary
care counselling across the PCT put out to tender. The
agency made the PCT aware that if they lost the contract
for the practices it would have a very damaging effect on
the finances of the agency. The PCT was also aware that
the counsellors used by the agency to work in the practices
received a lower rate of pay than the other counsellors.

The Mental Health Trust was keen to incorporate the
primary care counsellors into their psychology department, and to use the psychology department manager
to manage the counsellors. The independent counsellors
were very concerned as they thought the psychology
service would not understand counselling and that
they would have to retrain as cognitive–behaviour therapists.

In many such cases the management, and in particular
the clinical protocols, of a secondary service-run counselling provision have been more suited to psychology or
psychiatric approaches to mental health. These are not the
same as that of counselling or psychotherapy. This may
come as a surprise to some readers but is an important
consideration in setting up psychological therapy services
in any part of the NHS. It is not useful to reproduce
secondary care models in primary care. In certain cases
there has been ignorance as to what a professional counsellor is and confusion between counselling skills and full
professional training in counselling and psychotherapy.
This has given rise to poor terms for the counsellors and
muddled person specifications leading to the employment

of non-qualified personnel in counselling posts. It has also led to CPNs and psychologists not sufficiently trained in psychological therapy being expected to deliver such treatments.

Just to make things even more complicated, the GPs were very anxious that they would not lose their independent counsellors, whom they regarded very highly. Some managed counselling services have been formed directly from individual primary care practices and have been designed within primary care trusts themselves, These are based on a team approach derived from the generalist, non-emergency model of primary care wherein the primary care counsellor has been incorporated into primary care provision and into the primary care team itself. This has resulted in good team-working in many cases, with co-ordinated care for patients and good collaboration between GPs, counsellors, and other primary health professionals. On the downside, such services have often been marginalized from mental health planning and strategy from within the mental health care trust.

The heart of the matter

So, looking at Central Anywhere PCT's dilemmas, we can see that there are many variations on the organizational setting for a counselling service and, subsequently, an integrated psychological therapy service. No single model necessarily emerges as the front-runner. It is essential to consider the core ingredients for best practice and good organization and then apply them to the local model and needs. What is important is that the management model should understand the distinctness of professional psychological therapy (counselling and psychotherapy), which are disciplines in their own right and which pertain to a particular clinical treatment approach based on the therapeutic alliance. This is quite different from the skills and tasks of generic mental health workers and psychologists.

Furthermore, primary care counselling therapy involves a general therapeutic approach, which can and does apply to a wide range of people. The question that really needs to be considered by referring health professionals and service users themselves is more 'How suited is this person to using therapy?' than 'How ill is this person?' We liken this to a graph of psychological awareness/insight/motivation on the one axis and change versus severity of symptoms/illness/disturbance on the other. Patients who will make the best use of therapy could well be quite 'ill', but able to change with the right help and the right relationship. Similarly, some people with quite low-level mental health problems are unsuited and ill-disposed to therapeutic work.

Contrary to a lot of received opinion, counselling and psychotherapy in primary care offers both brief and longer-term therapeutic contracts to deal with a very wide range of presenting problems in a range of personality types and social groups. Far from working with just 'the worried well', counsellors and psychotherapists in the NHS work with very complex cases. In a way they mirror the work of their GP colleagues – they are specialist generalists. They undertake high levels of clinical assessment and treatment in a complex setting. For these reasons, whatever management frame is in place for the psychological therapy or counselling service in your locality, it is

important that management arrangements are implemented that are consistent with the principles of best
therapeutic practice and clinical support.

Moving forward

Back to our PCT; having considered their options the
PCT decided to look in detail at two of the four options
identified:

- a PCT-based service, with a counselling service
  manager and the counsellors employed by the PCT;
- a Mental Health Trust-based service, with a counselling service manager and the counsellors employed
  by the Mental Health Trust

Each option tackles the inherited difficulties within a
managed framework while adhering to the principles of
clinical governance and equity of access.

The key points for a PCT-based service were as follows.

1. Counsellors would continue to be GP practice based.
2. Counsellors would receive referrals within the GP
   practice and would assess the patient.
3. The counselling service manager would be employed
   by the PCT.
4. Primary care needs would be paramount.
5. There would be equity of provision across the PCT.
6. The Counsellors would be employed on an equitable
   basis using Agenda for Change job profiles.
7. There would be as minimal disruption for existing
   practitioners as possible. Human Resources would be
   involved throughout the process.

8. The service would be managed out of the Patient Services Directorate of the PCT.

The key points for the Mental Health Trust based service were as listed below.

1. Counsellors would be based in three locality centres.
2. All referrals would be sent to a central point, where an assessment team would allocate them to an appropriate worker.
3. The counselling service manager would be employed by the Mental Health Trust.
4. There would need to be a learning curve to understand primary care needs.
5. The counsellors would be employed on an equitable basis using Agenda for Change job profiles.
6. There would be as minimal disruption for existing practitioners as possible. Human Resources would be involved throughout the process.
7. The service would be managed out of the Psychology Department in the Mental Health Trust
8. All counsellors would be required to be trained in CBT.

After further discussion with the counsellors, GPs, practice managers and PCT staff, the decision was taken that the service would be based within the PCT, with a new counselling service manager being appointed. The manager would be tasked with setting up a service with employed counsellors. The key reasons for the decision were the Mental Health Trust's proposal to move away from GP practice-based counsellors and the move to central assessments, which the PCT believed would lead to unnecessary delay for patients and a fear that the Mental Health Trust might not understand primary care and its needs. However, it did recognize that close working links with the Mental Health Trust were essential.

The first step on that road was the appointment of a counselling service manager. It had been decided that this would be a full-time post, as the manager would line-manage all the counsellors and supervisor/s plus the half-time administrator. At this stage, there was not the funding available to appoint locality managers, who could have shared the management load.

Now let us introduce you to our cast of characters:

Linda: Primary Care Commissioning Manager, has had counselling on her action list for the last two years.

Alison: Newly appointed Counselling Service Manager, following an external review of the counselling provision.

Margaret: Director of Patient Services.

Simon: GP – PCT Mental Health lead, very pro counselling.

Stephen: GP – has a counsellor, but never really understood what it is all about.

Barbara: Counsellor – worked in her surgery for ten years, was the first counsellor there.

Karen: Counsellor – started in a surgery eighteen months ago, completed an additional training in primary care counselling.

We would emphasize that these are completely fictitious characters and based on no actual person, alive or dead!

Cherchez la femme/l'homme

Just appointing a counselling service manager proved problematic for Linda. She used the consultant to advise her on the job description and decided to advertise locally and in the journals of CPC and BACP, plus their websites. She was advised that the best place to advertise nationally was in the Society Section of the *Guardian* on Wednesdays, but didn't have a big enough advertising budget to afford it.

Linda also learnt that counsellors have traditionally been trained to work in private practice or voluntary agencies, and only recently have courses been established to train counsellors to work in particular settings. Courses for supervisors are in place and now courses for mentors and coaches are blossoming, but there is not much activity in the management of counsellors' arena. That could be for a number of reasons, the most obvious being that there aren't that many management jobs available. However, that is not necessarily the case. We know that there are 302 Primary Care Trusts in England, twenty-two Local Health Boards in Wales, and fourteen Health Authorities in Scotland. There are counselling centres in most towns in the UK, with Relate and MIND being major players in this field. In addition, there are hundreds of workplace counselling services in operation.

So, a reasonable guestimate would put the potential figure at about 1000 counselling service manager posts. However, support and training for those in post could be described as minimal (if we are being generous) to non-existent. In addition, in many instances the need for the post is unrecognized and it is therefore unfilled.

Linda wondered about this. Could the lack of counselling managers be due to the fact that it is a new profession and the recognition of the need for training of
managers just hasn't caught up? Certainly, but there
are also other questions to consider. These merit some
exploration as they have bearing on the task facing Alison
– our new manager.

- Do counsellors want to be managed?
- Do senior management think they need to be
  managed?
- Do counsellors believe they are competent to become
  managers and do they want to?
- What does a counselling service manager do anyway?

To manage or not to manage?

So, starting with our first and very fundamental question
– 'Do counsellors want to be managed?' On the whole the
answer is probably not. We have a group of counsellors
working in the NHS of whom most have taken up counselling as a second career. Many of these counsellors were
pioneers, the first counsellor in their surgery, coming from
the voluntary/private sector. They were self-employed,
and often isolated from the primary health care team.
They all believe passionately in the effectiveness of the
counselling they could offer. The vast majority were
trained to offer 'open-ended' counselling and struggled to
adapt to limitations imposed upon them. These limitations concerned the number of sessions counsellors could
offer to patients and the decisions as to the number were
usually made by non-clinicians driven by issues of funding
and also, possibly, of control.

Our second question was 'Do senior management think they need to be managed?' and again on the whole the answer would be an ambivalent 'Maybe'. This can be understood when we look at the history. Primary care counsellors were originally employed on self-employed contracts paid for clinical contact time only. A pretty cheap option at £20 an hour – especially when many counsellors never, or rarely, received a pay rise. Then the advent of primary care commissioning and equity of access resulted in the next logical step – a managed service. And managed services, done properly, are not cheap. Suddenly, going from independent counsellors to a managed service meant thinking about a lot of new things such as:

- employing a manager;
- employing an administrator;
- paying the counsellors for administration time;
- setting up a training budget;
- paying for supervisors;
- paying travel expenses.

That little lot doesn't come cheap. Much of this, if it had been considered at all, had previously been hidden by independent self-employed counsellors 'managed' by individual practices.

Whyever would we need to start wasting precious money on managers, when all we really need are good clinicians? Well, how do we know that they are 'good' clinicians might be a good starting point as a rationale for good management!

Providing effective treatments in the NHS is complex and based on a number of factors apart from the availability of 'good' clinicians. Notwithstanding this, many of the questions central to good management lie at the heart of such an apparently simple plea for 'more good clinicians'.

If we unpack the statement 'more good clinicians' things start to look less simple and aspects of management emerge.

How do we decide what a good clinician is? This implies questions about selection, qualifications, training standards, recruitment, professional standards, audit and evaluation, etc.

Who does the 'good' clinician see for treatment, when, where, for how long? This implies questions about clinical process, referral criteria, clinical protocols, assessment, risk assessment, clinical collaboration.

How do we know they are 'good'? This implies questions about outcome measurement, effectiveness, efficiency, safe ethical practice, personal appraisal, complaints and disciplinary procedures, supervised practice, and audit and evaluation.

How much is 'more'? Here we have questions about capacity, workforce planning, strategic planning, career development, and last but not least, more money!

Who decides they are good? This involves questions about experience, seniority, leadership, career pathways, increasing knowledge, management training.

So, as you can see, even a simple statement is loaded with management implications.

Our third question was 'Do counsellors believe they are competent to become managers and do they want to?'

The answer is, only a few. However, it is more complex than that. Counselling is about equality, empowerment, and being non-judgemental. It is not about disciplining poorly performing staff or being attacked by colleagues who do not understand counselling and, indeed, can feel threatened by it. It is not about budgeting, administration and politics, which is what every manager has to do. So, for a counsellor to step into a management role the issues are not just about ability but also about being able to sit comfortably in two different places.

Our final question was 'What does a counselling manager do anyway?' We hope that the following list will give some idea of the areas that need to be covered. A managed service requires:

- standards;
- accountability;
- clinical governance;
- audit and evaluation;
- referral criteria;
- budgets;
- protocols;
- legal and ethical practice;
- equal opportunities;
- performance data;
- workforce planning
- career development
- training – continuing professional development;
- research – evidence base.

And if ever we saw a list of good management words – there they are!

In this book we will work through each of the above and demonstrate why structures need to be in place to ensure that the counsellors you employ are safe, effective practitioners, that you know how many patients they are seeing, for how long, and what the clinical outcomes are. That the service gives and gets value for money and that the counsellors are managed and supported. For the counsellors, it is important to discuss transparently what it means to be managed. The following words are all relevant to being managed:

- supported;
- co-ordinated;
- appraised;
- facilitated;
- directed;
- disciplined.

To a great extent it depends on background and experience as to any individual's understanding of the concept of management and whether or not s/he thinks it is a good thing.

Providing effective treatments in the NHS is a management task as well as a clinical task. It is necessary to make sure that the proper arrangements are in place for safe and effective treatments and that the different parts of the system work together. It is also necessary to ensure that financial and human resources match up and that the treatments are provided by skilled, effective personnel who know what they are doing and who are supported. To do so we need checks and balances along the way to ensure that all is going as well as can be expected.

Counsellors and the NHS
– strange bedfellows?

We have outlined the case for the management of a clinical counselling service in general within the context of broader psychological therapies. We have seen that there are different implications depending on where the service is managed. But there are also different implications depending on the actual clinician. As we have stated, many counsellors working in the NHS have taken up counselling as a second career. They have been trained in the provision of longer term therapies. The nature of the setting of general practice had a great impact on the level of collaboration and confidentiality they could expect. The constraints within the NHS also had an impact on the amount and type of therapy they could offer.

As such, the cohort of independently minded counsellors and psychotherapists that has grown up in the NHS over the past twenty years proves to be a very different kettle of fish from dyed-in-the-wool NHS colleagues trained and schooled within NHS mental health and primary care – nurses, clinical psychologists, CPNs, etc. When it comes to management and integration, such counsellor clinicians are not necessarily the usual model for the NHS clinician. Nor are they necessarily the stuff of which NHS managers were once made.

However this non-medical independence of thought has had both good and bad consequences. Practice counsellors and psychotherapists have proved to be both difficult to manage and capable of great resourcefulness and flexibility. Out of this evolutionary material have come today's counselling service managers and integrated psychological therapists, all of whom learnt on the hoof, but there is a game of catch-up taking place all the time. Their psychology colleagues and other mental health professionals in primary care more often find themselves in the mainstream of mental health planning and policy and higher up the pay scales, despite the counsellors' long years of training and experience in the field.

Again, when we look at the history, primary care counsellors were originally employed on self-employed contracts paid for clinical contact time only. A pretty cheap option at a straight fixed rate of an average of £20 an hour. By comparison, a clinical intervention by a clinical psychologist or secondary service psychotherapist would come in at over £100, with all the associated on-costs, etc.

At the same time it means counsellors thinking about what being managed might mean for them, such as:

- support;
- appraisal;
- responsibility;
- co-ordination;
- facilitation;
- direction;
- clinical representation and lobbying;
- discipline;
- guidance;
- organization;
- leadership.

Something for everyone there!

Whatever the decision, introducing new management structures costs money, results in change for the primary care organization, mental health services, and clinicians.

Pros and cons of management change

The table sums up the consequence of such management change in terms of gains and losses for both the counsellor and the primary care organization.

Gains	Losses
PCTs	
Improved patient choice	
Standards	Takes time
Measurement	Takes money
Support	Can cause problems with GPs
Increased clinical resources	Can cause problems with secondary services
Clinical governance	Investment in specialist clinical/ managerial knowledge
Accountability	
Equity of access to therapeutic treatments	
Counsellors	
More inclusion, less isolated	Loss of autonomy/independence
Supported	Lack of control
Improved job security/ fixed income/pay scales	Flexible hours/money
Represented	
More status and recognition	Structure imposed
Appraised	Less clinical freedom
Training opportunities	
Career development	

On balance it is hard to come down either way in terms of gains and losses. However, without question if counselling is going to remain in the NHS and have the necessary clinical impact it must now be driven by a managed model.

How much change arises as a result of restructuring and how much this costs depends on the pre-existing local configurations and the future service plan. How successful you are in bringing about much needed change depends on the skill and will of the personnel involved and the relationships between health partners.

What is crucial to success is that the managed service is integrated within local configurations in order that:

- counselling is no longer regarded as optional;
- counselling is understood as a distinct psychological therapeutic provision;
- clear referral protocols and integrated referral pathways are established – counsellors should not work out in the cold nor be marginalized within the NHS;
- counselling services need their own management and professional representation.

To quote the DoH's paper, *The Organisation of Psychological Therapies* once again, there are

> widely different rates of pay and terms and conditions for those delivering psychological therapy which includes counselling. At the same time demand for psychological therapies is high and such approaches are extremely popular with service users and carers. [DoH, 2004]

Thus, it behoves us to ensure that we get the provision in at the right level with the right structures in place to ensure continued best practice in counselling and other psychological therapy services.

CHAPTER THREE

MAKING IT HAPPEN!

Outline and aims

This chapter discusses the steps required to create a co-ordinated, managed primary care counselling service. This guidance could as easily be applied to a voluntary counselling agency, or a new business start-up of a counselling provider.

* * * * *

In the previous chapter, our primary care commissioning manager, Linda, was getting much closer to being able to remove 'sort out counselling' from her to-do list. She had the go-ahead to employ a counselling service manager and to move to an employed service. She worked with the consultant and produced a job description and person specification for a primary care counselling service manager (Appendix 1).

Open and honest – the way to go

Linda was very aware that if this was going to be success-ful, then transparent communication with the existing stakeholders was absolutely essential. The independent counsellors, the Mental Health Trust, and the voluntary counselling agency had all been part of the service review carried out by the consultant. The next step was to communicate the results to all involved. Accordingly, meetings were set up to inform everyone of the next steps. Initially, Linda had thought she would write to everyone, but realized that for the voluntary counselling agency in particular, this was going to be seriously bad news, and decided that meeting face-to-face would be preferable (if daunting).

Deciding that there was safety in numbers, Linda and the consultant met with the counselling agency. While it was not the easiest of meetings, a way forward was achieved. The strengths of the agency were in longer-term counselling and in training. It was made clear that the primary care counselling service would be offering brief counselling interventions in GP practices. While there was no funding available to support the counselling agency at this stage, the possibility of the agency putting forward a proposal to the PCT to provide longer-term counselling was discussed and agreed.

More immediately, plans for the counselling service to include a training placement scheme were discussed. The proposal was that an agreement could be reached with the agency that would provide their student counsellors with workplace placements within the primary care counselling service. Again, this would not take place immediately, but was recognized as a major step forward in a professional approach to providing training placements for student counsellors. Linda heaved a sigh of relief at this development. She had a file full of letters from student counsellors asking for placements in GP practices and had no idea what to do with them. In fact, she had been quite taken aback by a few very angry, anxious students quite desperate for a placement to gain work experience. She thought it very odd that the students had to find their own placements and didn't understand why proper schemes weren't in place.

One meeting down and two to go!

The next meeting was with the Mental Health Trust. This again was a trifle tense. The head of the psychology department was extremely disappointed that the service would not be run out of the Mental Health Trust and very concerned as to what would happen to the four counsellors employed by the department. Linda made it clear that the funding the PCT had provided to the Mental Health Trust for primary care counselling would be withdrawn. As the Mental Health Trust employed the two counselling psychologists and two cognitive–behavioural therapists, the PCT would have to consider whether it wished to offer them employment in the new managed counselling service and how their skills would fit into the new structure. The PCT was also aware that under TUPE (Transfer of undertakings (protection of employment) regulations) their earnings would be protected for the next year. The consultant was a little anxious at this point; she suggested that it was important that all potential counsellors should be interviewed for this new service. From experience she knew that there were counsellors working up and down the country with some fairly minimal qualifications, if any at all. In this case, it would be important to ensure that the counselling psychologists and cognitive–behavioural therapists would fit into the new service. It was agreed that the Human Resources department would be consulted as to the proposals and the correct way to proceed.

The final meeting was with the independent counsellors. This went quite well, much to Linda's relief. The counsellors knew that the move to employment was inevitable and were pleased that they were going to be employed by the PCT. However, there was some confusion as to what this would mean and whether they would lose out financially. For some of the longer-established counsellors there was strong resistance to returning to employed status and even more to being 'managed'. Their view was that it all worked fine at the moment and 'if it ain't broke, don't fix it!' For Barbara, who had worked in her surgery for ten years, this was all quite threatening. She kept hearing about audit and evaluation, outcome measures, and evidence based practice – she didn't actually fully understand what any of those really meant but was worried that she would be asked about the way she worked and what results she achieved. She knew people liked to talk to her and was sure that it helped them. She found it difficult to explain what she actually did with her clients but knew that it worked.

Other counsellors held a very different view; Karen, who had started as a primary care counsellor only eighteen months ago, was delighted. Counselling was her profession; she was ambitious, keen to be able to move up a career ladder, and saw this move as the beginning of that process.

During the meeting Linda explained about the procedures for appointing a new counselling service manager. She invited the counsellors to consider whether they might wish to apply for the post and reassured them that the manager would be a counsellor, ideally with primary care counselling and management experience. Barbara could not think of anything worse than being a manager;

Karen considered it very seriously but decided that she did not have enough experience at that time to apply.

Linda went ahead with advertising in the local press and circulated the advert to all the existing stakeholders. Then she held her breath while she waited to see how many applications she got and whether they were any good.

Much to her relief, she received twenty-one applications. She worked with the consultant to produce a short-list of five. They used the person specification and job description, with a scoring system, to ensure that the candidates met the specification as closely as possible. Unfortunately, no applicant had all the relevant experience. Linda and the consultant had been aware that this was predictable, as there has been virtually no provision of management training for counselling managers.

Linda had involved Human Resources in the process from the beginning, to ensure that correct procedures in terms of both the PCT and employment law were followed. A member of the Human Resources department joined Linda and the consultant to form the interview panel for the post. The panel had a pre-meeting to prepare for the interviews. They decided to use a competency-based approach, identifying five key skills that they believed were key for this post. These were:

- communication and teamwork;
- planning and organizing;
- adaptability;
- management;
- strategic thinking.

The panel particularly wished to explore the applicant's abilities both clinically and managerially. As discussed in the previous chapter, this mix could be difficult to find.

Two candidates out of the five were possible for the post. John had strong managerial experience from his first career, had retrained as a counsellor and worked in the voluntary sector. Alison was a primary care counsellor in a neighbouring PCT. She had organized the counsellors in her PCT into a cohesive group and was battling away to get the counsellors integrated into the PCT. While she lacked formal managerial experience, the panel decided that she had demonstrated the relevant skills in setting up and leading the counselling group. They also valued her knowledge of the NHS, the National Institute for Mental Health, England (Nimhe), NICE, and the national issues surrounding primary care counselling.

After much deliberation, Alison was offered the job.

First steps

Alison started in the new post three months later. She was located in the PCT offices and reported to the Director of Patient Services – Margaret. This directorate was responsible for the delivery of patient services such as health visitors and district nurses. It made sense for the counselling services to be located in the same directorate, where the relevant skills and expertise were available. Linda, the primary care commissioning manager, heaved a huge sigh of relief and returned to the mountain of paperwork on her desk. Reflecting on the whole process, she wondered why such a small group of counsellors and such a very small budget could have taken up so much of her time.

Alison had been busy in the three months' notice period from her previous job. She had been looking for guidance from colleagues, reading relevant material from her professional bodies, and familiarizing herself with Department of Health documentation such as:

- The National Service Framework for Mental Health and its updates;
- Organising and Delivering Psychological Therapies;
- relevant research;
- NICE protocols: depression, generalized anxiety;
- evidence-based guidelines.

When she arrived at the PCT, she was presented with an induction programme. This covered the following areas:

- PCT structure – meetings with relevant personnel;
- briefing by the consultant as to the review results;
- meeting with Margaret – Director of Patient Services;
- meeting with Simon – GP, PCT Mental Health Lead;
- meeting with Pam, half-time administrator;
- meeting with counsellors.

Alison decided that, among her first tasks, it was essential for her to get to know the counsellors and to understand their concerns and fears about the move to employment. She was apprehensive that she might be seen as 'the bad guy' and wanted the counsellors to be aware that she would be very supportive of them and would ensure that they were offered good terms and conditions of employment.

Action

Alison started to work up an action plan. This needed to include the following points.

1. Allocation of counselling hours per surgery. (Up till now the counsellors had only been paid for their clinical hours. For part-time counsellors, it had been agreed that there should be a 60/40 split between contact and non-contact time: 60% contact and 40% non-contact.)
2. Clear understanding of the budget.
3. Termination of existing contracts (giving required notice).
4. Drawing up of a service specification (to include all relevant protocols and training and experience standards for counsellors).
5. Drawing up a grading profile for posts (this would reflect existing post-holders, but would give the flexibility in future to employ entry level counsellors). This would result in a spread of grades of counsellor, career progression, and succession planning.
6. Agreeing pay and conditions, using Agenda for Change bandings for counsellors (Appendix 1).
7. Advertisements for new posts (guarantee to all existing post holders of an interview, providing they met the required training standards).
8. Decision as to minimum/maximum number of hours a counsellor would work. (This was a tricky area for Alison. Twenty-five practices did not necessarily mean twenty-five counsellors. At the moment there were

twenty practitioners providing primary care counselling, of whom one worked three hours a week and
another five hours a week with four practices without
a counsellor. Alison was aware that it was easier to
employ fifteen counsellors, some working in more
than one surgery, than to employ twenty-five counsellors – one for each surgery. However, she was also
aware that counselling was often a part-time profession, with counsellors working for different employers
through the week, also offering supervision and training and usually with a private practice as well. Alison
knew that it was a time of change for the counselling
profession. She wondered if, in five years' time, the
norm would be for full time counsellors to work in
the NHS, seeing 20–22 patients during part of the
week and using the rest of the time for supervision,
clinical case consultation, meetings, training, mentoring, etc. This was the model operated by other health
professionals.)

9. Decision as to how supervision would be incorporated into the service. (Alison was also aware that this
was a very sensitive issue. Up till now the independent counsellors had their own supervisors, the PCT
had no idea who they were. It had been agreed that
supervision would be part of the managed counselling
service but decisions had to be taken as to how much
supervision, how many supervisors and whether it
would be individual, group or both.)

10. Urgently meeting with Human Resources and the
head of the psychology department to discuss the
issues concerning the two counselling psychologists
and two cognitive–behavioural therapists.

Falling into place

Gradually the pieces of the jigsaw started to fall into place. A decision was reached that the psychology department would offer a CBT service that GPs and counsellors could refer into. This was not funded from the primary care counselling budget, which had been a bit of a battle for Alison. She had built a useful working alliance with Simon, the PCT Mental Health Lead, who understood the need for generalist primary care counselling to be available through each GP practice. They took a proposal forward that identified the allocation of counselling hours to each practice and ensured that the GPs and practice managers were kept well informed.

More action

After discussion with Human Resources, the following action plan was agreed:

1. All counsellors would be offered an interview with Alison, a Human Resources representative, and Simon. It was anticipated that the majority of counsellors would prove to be appropriately trained and would be offered a job at their relevant grade.
2. To cover the surgeries vacated by the psychology department staff and the four surgeries with no counsellor, it was anticipated that those counsellors who worked a very few number of hours would be able to take on some additional hours. It was hoped that the result would be no counsellor working less than two days a week.

3. The GPs would be invited to make any comments concerning the counselling provision.
4. Adverts would be placed for supervisors and interviews held.

In parallel to this, Alison was working away on the service design, which will be discussed in detail in Chapters Four and Five. As part of the service design, Alison had a budget for the introduction of the Clinical Outcomes Routine Evaluation (CORE). This is an audit and evaluation package used very widely in counselling services. (See Appendix 2 for a more detailed description of CORE.) She was concerned that so many changes were being introduced at once and anxious as to the impact this would have on the counsellors. She decided that she would ensure that all new procedures introduced would be compatible with CORE, and to phase in its introduction once the service was fully up and running.

Alison also had big plans for a trainee placement scheme to be set up in the service. However, at this stage there was no funding to pay for mentoring of trainees, so this was put on the back burner. Alison did include this as part of a bid for development funds in the next financial year. In fact, she thought it might be a very effective way to increase counselling provision without enormous additional costs.

Alison and Pam (the administrator) were working well together as a team by now. Pam had worked in the PCT and its forerunner, the PCG, and knew her way around the system. This proved invaluable for Alison as she tried to get to grips with her new role. She believed in effective networking and tried to identify the key personnel with whom she should establish a good working relationship.

Despite inevitable setbacks and problems along the way, six months later Alison emerged with fifteen employed counsellors, covering all the practices. The single-hander practice with no room at all had reached an agreement with a neighbouring practice that his patients could be seen there. The practice that never replied to any letters re counselling continued to prove elusive. In the end, in desperation, Alison just turned up and talked to the practice manager. Apparently, the GPs were facing some very difficult issues concerning their partnership and quite a few things were being ignored. It was agreed that a counsellor would be allocated to the practice, but would require particular support in setting up a service within the practice. Both Alison and the practice manager would provide this.

Getting the basics right

Alison was aware, from the consultant's report, that there were wide variations in procedures for contacting clients, managing waiting lists, and paperwork. Some counsellors rang patients, some wrote, some completed an opt-in form, some didn't; some sent out an information leaflet, some didn't! So, to bring some order to chaos, Alison worked out a flow chart (Figure 1), which set out a clear audit trail.

Sample paperwork is given in Appendices 4, 6 and 7.

Unsurprisingly, there were some mixed reactions to this. Barbara was beginning to feel quite fed-up. She felt that her work had been going on fine for the past ten years, but now she was employed she was having to fill in so many forms and she couldn't see any benefit at all.

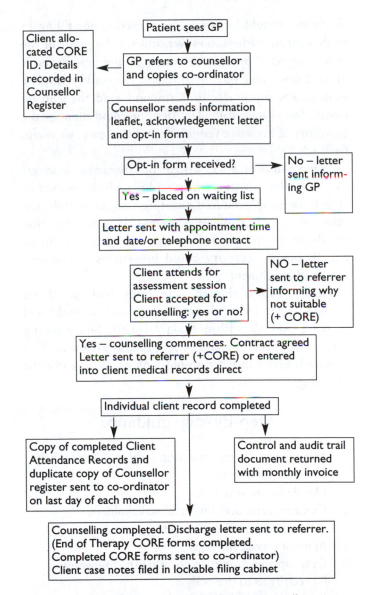

Figure 1. Procedural flow chart – primary care counselling service.

Surely she should be seeing more clients, not filling in endless forms. Others, however, did see the point of the tightening up of procedures. Karen got her head round it quite quickly and was delighted as she could complete most of the forms electronically and send them in by e-mail. She also liked the fact that she could monitor the outcomes of her work very easily and this gave her useful feedback.

Using e-mail provoked an anxious discussion amongst the counsellors about security on-line, which resulted in guidelines being produced ensuring that all confidential information was password protected. It was agreed that no identifiable patient information would be sent in an e-mail, but if necessary could be sent as a password protected attachment.

Finally, Alison thought she really had got there: employed counsellors, all practices covered, an audit trail in place and all within budget (just!). Summarizing Alison's experience, a step-by-step guide as to how to put a managed service in place would look something like the following.

Step-by-step guidance

1. Mapping of current provision – bring in expert help.
2. Involve all stakeholders.
3. Decide future structure.
4. Communicate decision to all stakeholders.
5. Advertise for service manager.
6. Appoint service manager
7. Draw up an action plan covering the following:
   (a) clarity as to the budget;
   (b) clinical/administration hours split;

(c) allocation of clinical hours to GP practices;

(d) termination of existing contracts;

(e) draw up a service specification;

(f) draw up a grading profile for posts – counsellors and supervisors;

(g) agree pay and conditions;

(h) decide minimum number of hours to employ counsellors for;

(i) advertise/interview for new posts – involve Human Resources and the GPs;

(j) develop specialist services, e.g., CBT, family therapy, etc.;

(k) draw up service guidelines and protocols;

(l) standardise procedures;

(m) introduction of CORE.

8. Sit back and relax (we jest!).

CHAPTER FOUR

DESIGNING A MANAGED SERVICE: STRUCTURAL ASPECTS

Outline and aims

This chapter outlines the structural, organizational and design elements specific to a managed counselling service in the primary care context. It explores areas such as workforce planning, service design, evaluation, accountability, budgeting, etc., in the real context of resource limitations and multi-professional clinical teams.

* * * * *

Getting there

OK . . . so you've read the first three chapters of this book and by now you'll have a rough idea of

- the development of primary care counselling;
- the need for counselling provision in primary care within the overall context of psychological therapies in the NHS as a fundamental part of mental health care best practice;
- the pros and cons of managing such services;

- where such services might best be placed depending on local conditions – in a primary care trust; with a private provider; in a secondary mental health trust or in a Portakabin on the M4!;
- the implications of the different models of provision;
- you may even know who is managing this service and, if luck and a prevailing good wind has it, they may well be someone with a counselling or psychotherapy training and clinical experience in the NHS.

But now the fun starts. Back to Alison, our dedicated, passionate, and very hardworking counselling manager, who now has to design and implement all the protocols for the new managed service. She also needs to get all the counsellors, mental health professionals and the PCT staff on side, fulfil the clinical parameters of the counselling profession and accord with government directives in clinical governance and mental health service frameworks and with a PCT that is usually otherwise occupied and often altogether unfamiliar with such service needs . . . is that the sound of running feet we hear?

The aims of the service

Before we begin to look at the detail required to plan a service that can offer easy access to appropriate, effective counselling provision to patients in primary care, it might be worth trying to identify what a managed counselling service needs to be. This in turn helps identify the 'how and what' of service design.

Thus, a managed counselling service in the primary care setting aims to:

- provide an accountable, cost effective, accessible service to all service users in the local population;
- provide appropriate, professional, rigorous, clinically effective and safe treatments in primary care;
- establish effective liaison with secondary and tertiary mental health services in order that all health professionals involved in mental health care communicate and co-ordinate their work with one another;
- enhance the current provision of primary care counselling in order that all adult service users within the Primary Care Trust have access to counselling in primary care;
- be efficient, maximizing treatment availability and high quality within available resources;
- promote integration within the primary care team and with other psychological therapy providers;
- provide counselling in primary care as a treatment option where appropriate, in keeping with DoH recommendations.

Service design

In order to achieve these aims the counselling service has to be designed according to realistic budgeting but also the resources needed for best practice – in other words you must cut your cloth accordingly. All aspects of service provision need to be considered and accounted for at the outset and the service expanded within agreed budgets. The structure that Alison was putting in place for the service is shown in Figure 2.

In a service to provide primary care counselling for a PCT the size of Central Anywhere PCT, it would be just

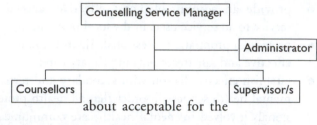

about acceptable for the

Figure 2. Alison's service design.

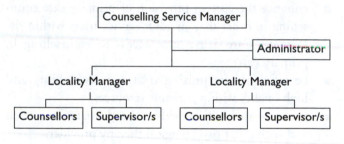

Figure 3. Service design for a larger PCT.

service manager to line-manage all the counsellors, the supervisor and the administrator. However, in a bigger PCT, the structure shown in Figure 3 would provide less of a flat structure.

Alison had identified a number of essentials in her service specification.

• All counsellors employed in the service are qualified and trained to minimum standards (see Chapter Five) and are able to undertake assessment, risk assessment, and to provide a counselling treatment and referral collaboration.

• Counselling supervisors, with relevant training and experience to supervise primary care counsellors, will be part of the service and will offer individual or group supervision (as required by the CPC's Code of Ethics).

- The clinical parameters of the counselling provision will be defined. At this stage the service will provide short focused, time-limited counselling interventions. Alison was very keen to expand the service to provide medium and long-term work. She recognized that budget realities meant there was no possibility of that at present, but she was determined to hold the vision and submit bids for future funding to expand the service. She was also very interested in group work and particularly keen to introduce family therapy provision. She recognized that a managed counselling service can be designed to offer a range of therapeutic interventions as long as the counsellors recruited are working within their training competences.

- For services operating within primary care, the service will establish and maintain regular liaison and clinical consultation with secondary mental health services, including psychiatry. (In such cases where the provider is an independent, private provider, then they should establish close working links with NHS mental health services and consultants and appoint a psychiatric consultant.)

- For a counselling service integrated within the departments of either psychology or psychotherapy, then it would be appropriate for a counselling service manager to be appointed and physically located within these departments.

An outline service specification is given in Appendix 3.

Service provision

Planning service provision needs to take into account the clinical requirements of the counsellor and also all the other aspects of NHS work that they are required to carry out within a complex multi-disciplinary environment. For too long counselling has been regarded as clinical contact time only, which has had serious implications for costing and workforce planning compared with other psychological therapy provision. In the past this has given rise to some very poor employment practice and poor counselling practice, often with no paid provision for non-clinical work and hence inadequate attention to good collaborative practice, clinical governance, and record-keeping. The counselling service is a major arm of the overall psychological therapy provision in today's NHS and, as such, the counsellors' work covers all aspects of clinical work, supervised practice, administration, team-working, co-education, training, professional development, etc. All of these aspects come in under service provision. The service needs to be able to provide the following.

1. Clear information about the service to colleagues and patients (through written information, induction training, regular meetings, audit and outcome feedback etc.).
2. Detailed initial assessment appointments to all referrals in the first instance in order to establish whether counselling is appropriate and, if so, what type/length, etc.
3. Ongoing counselling treatments as necessary.
4. Inclusion in integrated services – access to meetings, planning, etc.

5. Outcome measurement and audit.
6. Adequate records and notes.
7. Support and management of all personnel.
8. Waiting list management.
9. Staff appraisal.

Thus, the post of counsellor must be defined in terms of both clinical and administrative and team duties.

Let's take the above one by one.

1. *Clear Information*: Appendix 4 gives a sample information leaflet for patients. It may seem slightly odd to comment that perhaps fellow health professionals have less of an idea of what counselling means than the general public – but sometimes we wonder! To fully integrate a counselling service into primary health care, all health professionals need to understand what counselling is and how it works and all counsellors need to be able to explain what they do. So, written guidelines to referrers would be helpful, as would information meetings with all health professionals and feedback as to what makes a good counselling referral.

2. *Detailed assessment*: Assessment is the fundamental essential of primary care counselling. All clients need to be assessed as to whether the counselling intervention, with *this* counsellor at *this* time, is going to be helpful. Many counselling trainings do not include assessment, which is to be regretted. Alison must ensure that a top priority is to check that all her counsellors are trained in assessment and, if not, to provide some training urgently.

3. *Ongoing treatment*: Once a client has been assessed and it has been agreed by client and counsellor that a counselling intervention is appropriate, the counsellor will

then offer a number of sessions. These may be weekly, fortnightly, or monthly. The counsellor and client will work out between them what is the most helpful intervention. For some clients short sessions – thirty minutes each – may be better, for others a full fifty-minute session, but every other week, might suit. The key is that the counsellor is able to think flexibly and meet the clients' needs.

4. *Inclusion*: This has been a major problem for counsellors in the past. Too often there has been a group of independent counsellors with no paid co-ordinator or manager. Counsellors were not invited to planning meetings, were not included in strategic thinking, and were often forgotten. The paranoid among us may choose to believe in a conspiracy theory; more likely busy, busy people just do not have time to think about a group of practitioners who are sort of in but sort of out, of mainstream provision.

5. *Outcome measurement and audit*: CORE is the evaluation tool of choice for counselling. It has been designed for counsellors and supports their clinical and managerial activities. A detailed description of CORE is provided in Appendix 2 and there is further discussion on p. 82.

6. *Adequate notes and records*: Oh dear, what a minefield this proved to be! Linda, the PCT Commissioning Manager, could never understand all the fuss about notes; however, Alison could. She understood the difference between process and factual notes and the problems being faced whereby fear of involvement in litigation resulted in the counsellor writing notes defensively. Alison had attended a training day on 'Notes, Confidentiality and the Law', run by CPC, and was clear as to the complexities of the issue. To begin with, she instructed that all client notes must be kept in locked filing cabinets at GP practices.

She issued detailed guidance as to the period of retention and particularly addressed the question of how much detail should be entered in the patient's medical notes. (See Appendix 5 for more detail.)

7. *Support and management of all personnel*: Alison had spent a brief moment thinking that this was all very well, but where was her support? She calmed down when she remembered that CPC offered support specifically for managers, which guaranteed her immediate telephone advice, and also that her manager in the PCT was very supportive. She had involved Human Resources in the discussions about transfers from self-employment to employment and found their advice invaluable.

8. *Waiting list management*: Alison had strong views on this issue. She knew of some services where patients were referred to the counselling service and heard nothing till a letter arrived offering them an appointment the following week, sometimes after months of waiting. She set up a structure whereby the client received an acknowledgement of the referral, with information about the wait, an information leaflet, and an opt-in form. The client was asked to return the opt-in form and informed that if it hadn't been received within one month of the referral, it would be assumed that the client did not wish to take up counselling at this time and the referrer would be informed accordingly. (See Appendix 6 for sample forms.) If the wait was longer than indicated, the client received another letter informing them of the further delay and inviting them to discuss it with their GP if necessary.

9. *Staff appraisal*: One of the first tasks Margaret, the Director of Patient Services, had identified was to sort out

some training for Alison in staff appraisal. Alison was aware that CORE outcome evidence could also be used for appraisal of performance, and was seeking to get training in that area as well. She was also only too well aware that the preceding sentence might prove very threatening to some existing counsellors. She knew that the introduction of the concept would need to be handled sensitively, but was also certain that all staff need to be accountable and to be appraised as to the effectiveness of their work.

Presenting problems – whom to refer?

The service needs to be clear about its clinical aims and whom counselling is likely to help. As mentioned earlier, this is as much to do with the type of patient, their personality, insight, and motivation as it to do with what is thought to be wrong with them. A great deal can be done by counsellors to improve the effectiveness of their work through constant communication. This is best achieved through sensible, easy information given to health colleagues in the primary care teams and to patients themselves.

As a guide, the following could be considered 'suitable' presenting problems for a primary care service, but we cannot overestimate the fact that each individual needs to be considered in assessment.

- Difficult or long-term problems with grief and loss.
- Coping with injury or illness.
- Depression – reactive, circumstantial, and long-standing depression.
- Developmental or life crises.
- Emotional, physical, or sexual abuse issues.

- Relationship issues.
- General anxieties.
- Lack of direction, alienation, existential problems.
- Other losses, e.g., relationship, employment, health, etc.
- Self-image, self confidence and identity issues.
- Stress and trauma – pre and post event.
- Issues of sexuality.

The following may not be suitable for primary care counselling unless the counsellor has specific, relevant skills and/or is supported by the mental health services and specialist medical colleagues.

- Sexual dysfunction.
- Poor communication ability.
- Self-destructive behaviour which, over time, has shown very little change, i.e., prolonged substance misuse, eating disorders.
- Severe mental disorders.
- Severe challenging behaviours, i.e., aggression, violence, severe learning disabilities.

Referral guidance – knowing who will benefit

Following on from the notion of good communication with colleagues, it is also helpful to give some guidance to all potential referrers as to what other factors are good indicators of effective counselling.

- The patient's ability to change and their ego strength – this means their ability to tolerate the work done. The very fragile may well find counselling too challenging. On the other hand, those who have too much invested in remaining the same may also find counselling too challenging.

- The patient's capacity for insight – the ability and wish to think about themselves, to self-reflect and to move forward with new insights.
- The patient's ability to tolerate frustration – realizing all wishes cannot come true and the world is limited and not against them.
- The use of defences and the type of defences the psyche is employing.
- The capacity to make relationships.
- The degree of social support in the patients' personal and working lives. Counselling and psychotherapy can be a long haul for some and can affect people around the patient.

Any counsellor, whatever model they employ, should take a full history in the initial assessment appointment in order to ascertain whether this kind of treatment is going to be helpful. If colleagues know this they are less likely to set up unrealistic expectations for themselves and for patients. Counsellors may well, after assessment, re-refer the patient as inappropriate for counselling. They may suggest a referral to secondary mental health services or to another non-statutory agency if appropriate (e.g., specialist counselling services for abused women, bereavement services, etc.). Giving good, informed feedback to your GP colleagues is essential and respectful to all concerned.

Accountability

One of the major strengths of a managed counselling service is accountability. With counsellors and supervisors managed in one service, the referrer can be confident that all those involved are known, trained, and accountable to the service. This is not the case with individual private providers.

It is also useful to distinguish between clinical accountability and service accountability and to make an organizational model that ensures lines of communication exist and are used. For example, in primary care:

- the referring GP has ultimate clinical responsibility for his/her patients including those seen by the counsellor;
- the counsellor's manager has responsibility for the counsellor's professional conduct within the service protocols and within the NHS;
- The counsellor's supervisor has an important and individual role to play in terms of helping to clarify, probe, and guide the work taking place.

Whatever the organizational structure, it needs to enable all these parties to know their place and relate to each other. This can be done through regular meetings, collaboration on service design, and clear job descriptions that delineate roles for all concerned. Appendix 1 gives examples of typical job descriptions for service managers, supervisors, and counsellors.

Administration

The administration of the service also needs consideration. In the past this has been an area that has often been overlooked, particularly in the early days of counselling provision. This has meant that costs became muddled and extra burdens were placed on individual counsellors or practice staff for whom the work had not been clarified. If the service is incorporated into an integrated psychological service, then many of these administrative costs and tasks may well be incorporated, but they still need to be defined and they will have a significant bearing on costs and workforce planning. The main areas to be organized, planned, and time-managed are:

- rooms, privacy, resources for best clinical practice;
- reception/counsellor liaison – managing the appointment diary;
- letters, appointment systems;
- co-ordination and management of waiting lists;
- long-term sick – emergency cover;
- appropriate cross-referrals, pathways of communication;
- audit and evaluation;
- payment of staff;
- analysis of DNAs;
- organization of staff meetings/training workshops;
- standardized paperwork to be used by all counsellors (see Appendix 7):
  - (a) standard appointment letters;
  - (b) counselling information leaflet;
  - (c) client attendance record;
  - (d) client attendance summary;
  - (e) referral form;
  - (f) counsellor/client contract;
  - (e) discharge information.

Record-keeping, legal issues, and confidentiality

The important matter of record-keeping follows on from administration considerations. This is a thorny area for counsellors as it has implications for confidentiality and for how the counsellors' role is understood by their health colleagues and, more importantly, by the legal profession. Counsellors and psychotherapists are currently wrestling with the parameters and CPC is attempting to open up a dialogue with the Law Society in order to distinguish between civil actions and criminal actions and to discuss the expectation that counsellors should produce their notes if a solicitor/client asks for them. Under the Data Protection Act this is ultimately necessary *only if full informed consent has been given by the patient.* Service managers do need to ensure that all counsellors and supervisors are familiar with both the clinical governance requirements of the employing NHS Trust, Caldicott Guardian guidelines and the content of the Data Protection Act and can work within these parameters.

In practice, there can be tensions around the level of confidentiality expected by some health professionals as compared to counsellors. CPC has recognized that the code of confidentiality within the health service may need to be different from that of the private practice model wherein patient and counsellor hold mutual responsibility. The aim of CPC's work in this area is to ensure that, while the patient's confidentiality is ensured, this does not preclude good and necessary team-work for the care of the patient. To this end, CPC's Code of Ethical Practice (CPC, 2004) states:

4.1   CPC members respect the confidentiality and privacy of their clients, and work within the confines of the law.

4.2   Confidentiality varies according to the work setting. When CPC members work as an essential part of the Primary Health Care Team or in another NHS setting, for the successful health and well being of the client, some circumstances may occur in which the CPC member may wish to reflect the progress of a client's therapy with other members of the team who may be working with the client in parallel. It may therefore be appropriate for the counsellor to discuss with other members of the NHS team the process and progress of the therapy undertaken.

4.3   The personal content of the sessions with the client must remain confidential from other members of the specific team after due consideration of any legal requirements.

4.4   Any case material discussed within the team must not be taken outside of it without the informed consent of the client except within the confines of the law.

4.5   Clients should be informed of the confidentiality boundaries of working in a professional team, either verbally at assessment session, or in the form of an introductory leaflet. CPC recommend that clients should provide their written informed consent to the counselling process in accordance with the guidelines issued by the Department of Health.[1]

4.6   Where a client specifically requests a certain piece of information to be kept confidential from other members of the team, the CPC member may agree,

---

1.   Reference Guide to Consent for Examination or Treatment. DoH. 2001

providing that the information is within the jurisdiction of the law, and providing that its content does not reveal danger to the client, the counsellor, or to others.

4.7 CPC members must undertake risk assessment of a client who reveals an intention to self-harm. The client must be informed that this information may be shared with others members of the team who are also working with the client's health and well-being for prescribing or other therapeutic interventions.

4.8 CPC members must undertake risk assessment of a client who reveals an intention to harm others. CPC members must acknowledge openly to the client that this cannot be condoned, and that steps may be taken to break confidentiality in order to protect third parties.

4.9 CPC members have a duty to protect their clients from abuses of confidentiality in particular over access to the client's notes. They also need to protect themselves against abuses by clients who use the confidentiality ethic as a means of concealing their abuse.

4.10 CPC members must ensure that all records and notes of counselling sessions are kept secure and that authorised personnel can only gain that access to them in pursuance of the client's therapy.

To sum up this tricky area, the counsellor service manager has responsibility for ensuring the following.

● Counsellors are responsible for keeping adequate records as part of the patient's health records in accordance with the practice of their NHS Trust. Counsellors are responsible for the security of their own case notes, which are not part of the patient's records. These should be kept in a locked filing cabinet in the GP practice.

- Counsellors will keep a Client Attendance Summary, to include an assessment and discharge report, which will provide a brief, one or two sentence summary of each session – this is available to the client, if requested. It is only made available to others with the client's permission.

- Counsellors ensure their practice meets the requirements of the Data Protection Act. This is a training requirement of the service.

- Counsellors will be aware of relevant legislation, in particular:

  The Children Act, 1989;

  Prevention of Terrorism (Temporary Provisions) Act, 1989;

  Road Traffic Act, 1988;

  Data Protection Act;

  Consumer Protection Act.

- All counsellors and supervisors will have their own Professional Liability Insurance. NHS Trusts may vary in terms of the amount of coverage required.

Audit, evaluation, quality and outcome monitoring – or does it work, for how many and how much?

If you are not already defeated by all the aspects required to design and run a good service you may well be after reading this next section! As a service manager you are required to show that the work done is as responsible, safe, and effective as possible, both in terms of clinical effectiveness and cost effectiveness. Actually, this is not as bad as it may seem at first. A regular, straightforward audit system, together with an outcome monitoring system, can work as a useful management tool as well as providing very good material for service development lobbying.

Such systems should be able to provide information on the following key areas of the service (taken from Parry, 1992) in *Organising and Delivering Psychological Therapies* (DoH, 2004):

- Acceptability – does the service meet service users' requirements, are they satisfied with it, does it offer choice?
- Accessibility – is the service easily accessed by those in need and does it offer an appropriate range of interventions?
- Equity – is the service available equally to all those who need it irrespective of factors such as ethnicity, age, social class?
- Effectiveness – is it cost effective, maximising volume and quality within available resources
- Efficiency – is it cost effective, maximising volume and quality within available resources.

Ways of producing such information could be through regular monthly or quarterly monitoring to include:

- Number of Referrals
- Number of Assessments
- Number of Counselling Contracts
- Number of DNAs
- Number of Discharges
- Patient Profile Data

Collecting and analysing clinical effectiveness data is a more complex but a more interesting task. The CORE system (Mellor-Clark, Barkham, Connell, & Evans, 2000), was developed in 1998 to tackle the problem of using a standardized approach to quality outcome evaluation in the psychological therapies. It is now used widely across all tiers of NHS psychological therapy provision and particularly in managed counselling services. By comparing a patient's score using the standard questionnaires against reference data collected, a number of outcomes can be shown through the use of CORE:

- *Reliable and clinically significant change* – changes are unlikely to be due to chance and the patient's well-being and functioning has improved to move them into that which is regarded as similar to normal population;
- *Reliable change only* – changes are unlikely to be due to chance but their functioning is still lower than normal;
- *Clinically significant change only* – the change is clinically significant but the size of the change means that this might be due to chance;
- *Neither reliable nor clinically significant change.*

Interestingly, in a recent study of a fairly large sample of CORE data from counsellors in primary care nationwide, the following results were found:

Reliable and clinically significant change: 59%
Reliable change only: 17%
Reliable change: 1.5%.

A system such as CORE could be potentially useful as a benchmarking tool, either within a service or, as more services adopt it, across services. Data can be aggregated at the level of individual practitioner and therefore outcomes can be compared against waiting times, quality of referrals, etc., and similar services can be compared. This can be linked to overall management planning, e.g., with regard to waiting lists, which affects the take-up of counselling. We would stress, however, that the whole point of any sort of performance indicator is not to win prizes but to improve effective provision. If the performance indicators are not sensibly linked to planning there is little point in them.

Is that all?

Well, no actually – that's only half the story. In this chapter we have worked at structural aspects of service design such as:

- aims
- service design
- service essentials
- service provision
- presenting problems
- referral guidelines
- accountability
- administration
- record-keeping
- legal issues
- confidentiality
- audit and evaluation
- CORE

If that wasn't enough to be getting on with we now need to move to the clinical aspects of counselling service design. In Chapter Five we will concentrate on the specific clinical aspects of counselling service design – shall we press on?

CHAPTER FIVE

CLINICAL ASPECTS OF MANAGED SERVICE DESIGN

Outline and aims

This chapter explains the main clinical components of a managed counselling service – how they might be attained and implemented in terms of both the professional requirements of the counsellor and service protocols and design.

*   *   *   *   *

Questions, questions . . .

Before we even start the process of service design, from the point of view of what is clinically required, are we agreed as to what the counselling practitioner is, or should be, in today's NHS? Ten or so years ago, when primary care counselling began to emerge as a speciality, a practice counsellor was usually an independent practitioner employed by a practice on a self-employed, part-time basis. The counsellor could have been a fully trained counsellor, a psychotherapist, a psychologist, or a practice nurse who had done a weekend course in counselling skills. In what was then, and still is, an unregulated profession, such practice counsellors were variously trained in different modalities and not always to the same standard.

One strength of this evolutionary model has been the incorporation of the counsellor into the primary care health team with consequent benefits of working closely with referring GPs and other primary care health professionals – but, as we know, this can have its drawbacks too. GPs vary enormously as to the extent to which they buy into the effectiveness of psychological therapy *per se* and in the way they approach their work with practice therapists. Similarly, counsellors vary in their ability and willingness to work collaboratively within a medical paradigm.

With the advent of primary care commissioning, establishing managed counselling services became possible and, we would say, necessary. However, there have been inherent difficulties. Often the tensions in an individual practice over the management, funding, and effectiveness of primary care counselling have been transferred with renewed passion into the PCT or Mental Health Trust. In addition, there have been new tensions arising out of government directives as to the use of evidence-based treatments and clinical governance; all of this against the usual background of more resources and tighter budgets.

So, making it clear what a professional counsellor is, what she can do, what parameters she works within, etc., is fundamental to establishing a basis for a managed service in today's health service. That way you can take your service forward together with, not in opposition to, your colleagues, and in relation to health service directives on mental health policy. If you get the starting points right you are in a good place to go forward.

The perfect clinician – spot the difference

The profession of counselling is still not regulated by statute (unlike dentists or doctors or nurses). However, the professional bodies for counselling in the NHS, such as CPC, are self-regulating and have set training standards for registration. But there is still, as such, no protection of the term 'counsellor'. This, as we know, has led to confusion and difficulties in the workplace, particularly in the NHS, since many nurses and other health professionals have undertaken counselling skills' training alongside their core professional training. It is important to be clear about the difference between fully qualified counsellors and those who may use counselling skills as a useful adjunct to their work.

So what is a counsellor?

Alison, our counselling service manager, will have a very specific view of a what a counsellor is, which is based on an understanding of the clinical training required. Her perfect counsellor is:

- trained to an agreed standard commensurate with CPC Registered membership
- grounded in core theory plus NHS specialist training;
- experienced and trained in clinical assessment, time-limited work, and long-term work;
- experienced in working with a range of complex cases from diverse backgrounds and ages;
- knowledgable about mental illness and personality disorder;

- knowledgeable about NHS structures and primary care/secondary and tertiary interfacing;
- in ongoing supervision with a recognized supervisor with NHS knowledge and expertise and has undertaken personal therapy;
- working to a code of ethical practice relevant to the NHS;
- familiar with legal and ethical issues relevant to therapeutic work in the NHS. Keeps notes and records in line with practice/NHS requirements;
- graded and paid in line with Agenda for Change and on correct banding for training, experience, and job specification;
- confident and competent to discuss clinical matters with a range of health professionals (i.e., she can keep Simon, our modern GP, from interfering too much and involve Stephen, our retro GP, when possible!);
- organized and professional (i.e., submits her audits and evaluations without moaning);
- familiar with current research and willing to participate in research studies and evaluations;
- committed to relevant continuing professional development (CPD) on a yearly basis (thirty hours a year minimum);
- attends service meetings and contributes to development of the service in relation to joined-up mental health planning (i.e., doesn't just see patients).

Yes, that's all folks!

The NHS version

The PCT or Mental Health Trust may have other ideas. Their perfect counsellor:

- has received training (unspecified) in brief, low intensity, psychological therapy interventions;
- works with people with common mental health problems using an appropriate mix of self-help and time-limited, evidence-based therapy;
- works in accordance with NICE guidelines;
- works in accordance with locally agreed referral protocols and pathways;
- keeps adequate records;
- shows an interest in counselling and/or mental health;
- is good at talking to people;
- is undemanding;
- knows how to complete audits, to include waiting times;
- undertakes outcome evaluations;
- is cheap as chips;
- does what the doctors tell them to do

Simon, our enthusiastic GP, has his own views. Simon's perfect counsellor:

- is available at short notice to see patients he refers;
- keeps the waiting list to less than two weeks;
- uses evidence-based therapeutic interventions;
- follows practice guidelines;
- produces outcomes and audits;
- collaborates with GPs;
- keeps computer records up to date;
- is a good team worker;
- works to a strict time limit;
- lets him do a Beck score and/or other outcome measurement on the patients before and after they have been seen for counselling;

And Stephen, our other GP, thinks that *his* perfect counsellor:

● accepts all referrals sent;
● is a good sport at the Christmas party.

So, a bit of a difference in understanding here? Obviously these illustrations are deliberately provocative, but they are demonstrating a serious point: that there are still very wide gaps in knowledge as to what a primary care counsellor is; what professional counselling is; which patients can be helped; and how and what the role of the primary care counsellor is in the primary care team. Without a clear agreement as to this and, to some extent, an understanding of the need for the depth of training required, the demands on the practice counsellor from outside the therapeutic frame can cause chaos and a lack of safe practice.

Making it happen

Many an NHS manager may have little or no idea of what a counsellor or psychological therapist actually is or should be, and therefore finds it challenging to be involved in setting up a service specification for a counselling service. Their ideas may be vastly different from that which the profession regards as the minimum person specification for this highly complex and responsible work. Remember, the counselling profession has been its own worst enemy in keeping itself apart from other health professionals and in selling itself short in terms of taking unpaid work or low-paid work in a statutory service.

Therefore it is important from the start to set a minimum benchmark for training and qualifications and experience that is commensurate with that of the professional bodies and is real.

Managers and commissioners will welcome your input in setting high standards of best practice, since this is in keeping with their own aims of clinical governance and service evaluation. Remaining, together with your colleagues, steadfast in your collective obligation to the care of patients, citing current evidence-based practice and DoH guidelines, is the way to win hearts and minds on this one.

Authors' tip

It is important to be familiar with ever-changing government initiatives that will influence the shape of your service delivery. As we write, the most important frameworks and policies for you to get your heads round and for you to fashion your service delivery in relation to are given below.

- Clinical governance (CG). This is a key part of the government's modernization White Paper, *The New NHS: Modern, Dependable* (DoH, 1997), and relates to the way in which all NHS organizations are now accountable for the quality, monitoring, and improvement of the care they provide.
- *National Service Framework (NSF) for Mental Health* (DoH, 1999). This spells out seven standards for mental health, how they should be achieved, developed, and monitored. The aim is to improve quality of mental health care overall and reduce national variations in provision and quality.

- NICE. This was set up in 1999 to provide advice and guidance on best practice in all areas, including mental health. As we go to press there are a number of NICE guidelines that are directly related to the work of counsellors in primary care and in the NHS, e.g., depression; anxiety; eating disorders; bipolar disorder.
- The Commission for Health Improvement (CHI). This is an independent commission for the NHS that monitors implementation of the NSF standards and those of NICE, together with reviews of CG in all NHS Trusts – if you like it is the OFFWATCH of Health. You may already have been part of a CHI review in your PCT or MH Trust.
- The National Institute for Mental Health in England (Nimhe). This was set up as part of the government's new modernization agency within the DoH to be the key implementation vehicle for new mental health policy in England. Nimhe is organized into regional development centres and these centres are important contacts in terms of getting support for resources that underpin government policy in mental health, and for research, etc.
- The Association of Counsellors and Psychotherapists in Primary Care (CPC). This professional body was set up in 1998 to establish professional counselling in the NHS. They have guidelines and protocols on any aspect of counselling service design and clinical governance (CPC, 2004).

Within your PCT or Mental Health Trust there will be managers and clinicians who are intimately involved with the local, and possibly national, delivery of these policies and frameworks. Get to know them. Get to the meetings.

> Get psychological therapies in the framework and, most importantly, in the budget by using these directives to support the resourcing of your service to CG levels and NSF standards. Ensure all your counsellors are members of CPC and meet their standard. Join the national network of service managers. Find out where your local regional Nimhe centre is and use it and its resources. Network, network, network.

As the manager of the primary care counselling service you need to set the necessary clinical and health care standards in stone at the outset. You do this through:

- selection of personnel and design of job specifications for posts;
- overall organizational structure of the service – i.e., what skill mix and seniority mix you need;
- (most importantly for the purposes of this chapter) your framework of protocols for best practice. Get this sorted from the start and you'll be sunning yourself on a sabbatical . . . fudge it to suit the constraints and demands of others and it'll all end in tears, probably yours.

Aim high but be real

This is a hard one isn't it? You want the best possible provision but the NHS is not Utopia. It's an organization of huge need and finite, competing resources – or is it?

One of the many ways in which a 'good enough' managed counselling service can help the pressures on the NHS is the way in which limited resources are used to the best advantage. The benefits of a well set up service are not simply those to patients, although these are crucial, but to other health professionals and, more importantly, to the way we think about and manage our health care. We'll say more about this in Chapter Seven. For the moment it is worth considering whether to model your service as a gold standard and just start with a set of teaspoons, building it up over time, or to go for the whole cutlery set, including fish knives, in stainless steel right now! . . . these questions are worth pondering at the outset because they have a great bearing on the future long-term planning of the service and of the initial service design.

Our own feeling is that there are some things you can compromise on and some that you cannot. For example, you will accept that there is a limited budget, so you will aim to recruit personnel over a period of time. But you will not compromise on the actual person specification for such personnel nor, say, on the amount of clinical time versus administrative time they need to work.

A person specification was developed by all the leading professional bodies within the Counselling and Psychotherapy Training Forum for Primary Healthcare. These standards for a primary care counsellor are that of registered membership of the CPC. Employing counsellors *trained at least* to this level will result in recognizable quality counselling provision in the NHS, which would also accord with the clinical governance requirements of your Trust (see Appendix 1 for person specification for Band 5 counsellor). Not only that, but in employing personnel based on this specification you are ensuring that patients in primary care can get the sort of psychological therapy that they could benefit from with the least amount of fuss.

The levels set in this standard will not surprise many of you. Some may think it too 'lean'. Others may think it far too high. But remember this is a minimum training standard – many, many practitioners who work as counsellors and psychotherapists in primary care have undertaken far more extensive training than stipulated here, as well as many years of personal therapy, and of course continue with very high levels of CPD.

It is our feeling that such training should take a minimum of three years and maybe as long as five or six years all told. Counsellors are by necessity 'older' – they have life experience, gravitas. This is a must. Many counsellors have worked extensively in a previous profession for a number of years, not necessarily in a related field. All the competencies and experience they have gained elsewhere helps them attend with the kind of integrity and containment required for the job. It is tremendously important that psychological therapists working in the NHS are experienced and competent to work with a very wide range of patients, in a mixed provision of in-depth work. The specification recognizes an overlap and affinity between counselling and psychotherapy in this setting and that the psychological therapist working in primary care may well be both a counsellor and a psychotherapist or either, but above all must be highly trained as specified. On this note, the United Kingdom Council for Psychotherapy (UKCP) introduced a new section for 'Psychotherapeutic Counselling' in March 2004, which recognised this continuum.

So, as a manager – first things first – select practitioners who fit this profile. The rest is easy!

God is in the detail

Let us now assume you have recruited or inherited some appropriately trained personnel, and you have some idea of the shape of the service you can manage on the resources available, as well as an idea and a fiscal strategy for developing the service to optimum levels. Now we need to think about what this 'gold standard' service should provide, to whom, and how.

There are similar dilemmas in relation to service design as there are with respect to personnel standards discussed above. Do we spread ourselves thinly over as wide an area as possible, or do we work with a tiny, cherry-picked section of patients and ignore the rest of the world? One colleague in an NHS psychotherapy department talked of working 'in a clearing in the jungle' and of 'keeping the tigers out'! (The tigers were the NHS managers waiting to devour him and his service.)

How do we tailor what is often a very small piece of cloth to fit a best practice benchmark in terms of service protocols and treatment alliance aims when someone else has the scissors and is busy hacking away unmercifully?

Take, for example, the debate over the time-limited work versus longer-term work. It maybe more sensible and realistic in terms of resources available to set a limit to the number of sessions that counsellors can work with patients. In so doing you get reduced waiting lists (very good CHI!), happier GPs, and greater benefit to a greater number of patients. But you are also colluding with a myth that everyone in primary care is somehow routine and that we are the gatekeepers to more specialist work. Not so. General practice is full of complex, muddled, chronic cases, many of which avoid any diagnostic definition at all. And every GP or primary care counsellor today already knows this.

As the counselling manager you need to specify clear referral protocols to suit time-limited work in order that patients who can make use of this have relatively straight-forward access to it. At the same time, however, those needing longer-term therapy need to be identified in assessment and for their treatment needs not to be masked within the time-limited service. Without reasonable referral and assessment protocols there is a danger that practitioners will respond to waiting list pressure, arm-twisting due to lack of any other longer-term resource and to their own omnipotent fantasies, and try to shoehorn more complex cases into a time-limited frame. By putting protocols in place for time-limited work you can use the evidence of the numbers of patients assessed for longer-term therapy, and the outcome evaluations, to show that one size does not fit all and use this data as a way of arguing for more and different resources as necessary. The latter could then become a development plank of your managed service, given that you will already have counsellors who are trained to do long-term work. You also now have the ammunition to recruit further. Alternatively, the need for longer-term therapy could be met by a collaborative partnership with existing psychotherapy services.

So, when it comes to clinical aspects of service design, just as with the structural aspects described in Chapter Four, as a service manager you need to aim high but be real. Develop a flexible, responsive approach to all you work with, particularly your management colleagues, while setting out your stall with integrity, transparency and a close eye for detail. Build in regular checks and balances so that once the service is up and running it can be evaluated and monitored with no great effort. This can be beneficial rather than threatening if it is introduced at the outset. A routine evaluation measure such as CORE can be an excellent tool for a busy manager. Not only will this provide you with data on clinical outcomes from your service but also it will help identify training needs for individual counsellors.

Authors' tip

Belinda Wells, who manages a counselling service in South London/Kent, states:

> We use CORE PC2 in both services, and happily engage in the CORE benchmarking club. It allows us to review our service on a comparative basis with other time limited counselling services. We have a positive history of using CORE with a higher than average clinical and/or reliable improvement (currently at 85%) and lower than average waiting time (24 days) in one part of the service and 76% clinical and/or reliable improvement in the other part. . . . I now feel downright enthusiastic about statistics and computers and about applying them in a common sense way to our services. This helps me in my day-to-day work as a counselling service manager and identifying how best to develop the service together with the PCTs. [Belinda Wells, 2004]

Keep building

Building on the resources you have got is essential. It is very unlikely that you will have a full service in place when you start as a counselling manager, so outline what the gold standard version would be and work towards it. Establish a recruitment plan and a training programme for your existing counsellors and make sure this is specified in your service specification and in the budget. All counsellors and managers need to continue to develop professionally and in accordance with their clinical and NHS requirements. Training in the NHS for the psychological therapist will cover topics as wide ranging as legal aspects of record-keeping through to clinical assessment of personality disorder. The professional bodies require at least thirty hours of CPD a year for members, so this kind of training is a clinical governance requirement too.

Thus, the message is start as you mean to go on . . . and build on the core standards you have set for your service.

Authors' tips

Experience round the country shows that where services have been designed with protocols of practice in mind from the outset, standards and good practice have been much easier to achieve, because counsellors were recruited on this basis and are used to working accordingly. If you are managing an existing service that has not previously attended to these details, then start from scratch with everyone – that way you can say 'this is now' without comment on what was good or bad about what went before. This allows you to bring all existing counsellors into the best practice protocols and also recruit new staff to suit. Old hands may well be disgruntled, but if you apply the same standards to everyone and don't compromise with individuals you can carry the service. Get your management behind you, using clinical governance and the NHS White Paper to support you.

And what of our counsellors? How will they react to a new service manager who may well introduce service protocols that they are not so familiar with?

99

Barbara: 'I've been seeing my patients in my surgery for over ten years without having to refer to any protocols. I am a very experienced counsellor and I know how to assess patients. I need to be able to offer a patient as much therapy as they require – where else are they going to get this kind of help? My GPs know they can depend on me. It's no use referring anybody into secondary services – they just wait forever and never get seen.'

And Karen?

'I think these protocols will really help me . . . I've already been talking to my GPs about how to use my time in the surgery better – after all I'm only working eight clinical hours a week and there is plenty of time-limited work to do in that time. This way I can identify and refer on, either into private practice or NHS psychotherapy, those who I know will need longer-term work. If we keep accurate audits we can show whether we need to expand the service into medium and longer-term work in due course. Hmmm, I'd quite like a mixed practice myself in the future. I enjoy time-limited work but I am trained in long-term work, like all counsellors, and it would be good to have the mix in primary care. This would suit the needs of the practice too.'

Mixing it up

Given that you now know which clinicians fit the bill for employment in the NHS and what type of service you are offering, the next challenge is to design and structure your service. For the average PCT or Mental Health Trust, a psychological therapy service aimed at serving primary care will need to comprise four or five core elements:

- a service manager;
- psychological therapists (CPC registered counsellors; psychotherapists, or counselling psychologists) both senior, experienced, and newly qualified;
- supervisors;
- service administrator;
- counselling trainees on placement – optional.

Depending on the size of the population you are going to serve, the number of full-time equivalent posts and the seniority and skills mix required will vary. It is as well to design your service around the optimum structure first and then develop it according to budget limitations, aiming at building up to full service levels in due course.

The following points are essential in planning your service requirements (adapted from Foster & Murphy, 2004).

- The recommended provision of clinical counselling hours to patient population is two hours per 1000 patients – if you have less than this then your waiting list times will be longer.
- This assumes that counselling is an adult service (for patients over eighteen years). Counselling services for young people and children need to be differently defined and require further specification and specialist training and perhaps even managed in a different setting.
- Counsellors will be offering an initial assessment appointment(s) only to all referrals in the first instance, so this needs to be included in the clinical hours.

- Decisions need to be made as the range of work offered by the service. Most primary care counselling services offer time-limited work within the range of 3–18 sessions. However, you may elect to offer some longer-term work.

- Counsellors' time is divided into client contact time and administration. CPC recommend a ratio of 60:40 client contact to administration. The administrative requirements are substantial:
  - meetings;
  - record-keeping and notes;
  - evaluation and audit;
  - correspondence;
  - clinical collaboration;
  - service meetings and planning;
  - supervision.

- The total number of client contacts a week for a full-time counsellor should not exceed twenty-two and should ideally be around twenty maximum.

- Trainee counsellors on placement in a practice are not a substitute for qualified counsellors but are in addition. GPs do not take registrars into their practice to replace qualified doctors – the same is the case for counsellors and psychotherapists. Any trainee counsellor on a placement in primary care must work under an experienced, employed practice counsellor who acts as mentor and manages the placement.

The numbers' game

So, for a patient population of around 100,000 you will be looking for a mixed range of counselling experience from the senior manager to the newly qualified. If you fancy a bit of number crunching now you could look at this average service specification:

100,000 patients:	
at a ratio of two clinical counselling	
hours per 1000 patients, the total number	
of counselling hours per week would be:	200 hours
The number of full-time equivalents (fte)	
(counsellors) to provide this (max twenty	
clinical hours each per week):	10 fte

The mix of counsellors in this number should range from newly qualified to senior, the latter having mentor, training, research, and project management roles. The suggested range, using Agenda for Change bandings (see Appendix 1), could be:

Band 7 (specialist counsellor):   2
Band 6 (counsellor):   7
Band 5 (entry level counsellor):   3

Supervisors required to provide a minimum of 1.5 hours individual supervision per month (equivalent to 1.5 hr group of four counsellors per week)

Band 7   3 (part-time)

One full time clinical service manager

Band 8d   1

One full time administrative assistant: 1

The costings of such a service will vary depending on the ratio of whole time and part time counsellors, the pay scales at the time and the gradings of the range of personnel.

Alison was aware that she would probably have a different profile amongst the counsellors. This was because she was inheriting some long-standing practitioners and she anticipated that the service would be a bit top-heavy for a while, with a majority of counsellors at Band 6. As a number of these counsellors were coming up to retirement age, she planned to employ Band 5 (entry level counsellors) in their place. This would give a more even spread, reduce the wages bill and provide succession.

The latest model

One last note on staffing a service – what about the thorny issue of modality? Counsellors are trained and experienced in a variety of core theoretical models, ranging from CBT to psychodynamic. Many are also trained in integrative and eclectic models. So how do you plan your service, given that there is not only a range of experience but a theoretical range too?

The authors would like first to debunk the myth that counselling is based on a client-centred or person-centred model. Not so. In a typical service these days you will find counsellors and psychotherapists trained in any one of the several core models. As we have stressed above, what is important is not which model is used but how extensive is the original training, skills, and clinical experience. In fact, what emerges in reality is that the more experienced the therapist, assuming they continue to work and to develop, the more flexible she is likely to be while still working from her core training. Through additional learning, growing in clinical confidence, extensive supervision, sharing knowledge with others, continuing training and development, research, etc., each counsellor becomes a skilful and confident clinician. Confident enough to know how to do her work and to know her limitations.

If you are looking to recruit counsellors to work in primary care you want someone who:

- is initially very well trained and very familiar with her own core theory;
- is confident enough to know how to do her work and to know her limitations;
- can seek the help and support of others as well as to be available to offer it;
- is thirsty for knowledge and keen to grow in experience;
- can make good relationships.

A recipe for success – Primary Care Surprise

So let's take a detailed look at what a realistic managed counselling service would look like today. What elements does it need to contain to work, to offer best practice, and to develop? What's the recipe for success?

Catering for a PCT of 100,000 patients

INGREDIENTS

- One full/time counselling manager or head of service. Agenda for Change Band 8/9.

- Four experienced counsellors (between twelve hours to full-time each). Agenda for Change Bands 6–7.
- Four freshly recruited counsellors. Agenda for Change Band 5.
- Four part-time supervisors – primary care knowledge essential. Agenda for Change Band 7/8.
- One full-time administrator.
- One willing PCT commissioning manager (if this is not available you could use a mental health lead or director of primary care or commissioning, although the latter are rarely available and are often out of season!)
- GPs, CPNs, GMHWs, specialist psychotherapists and psychologists as available for added seasoning and pep!

EQUIPMENT

- A budget – for personnel, service costs, training, evaluation and research.
- A counselling manager, who is fully paid, trained in management and supported and managed herself.
- Counsellor person specification.
- Recruitment criteria.
- Pay and conditions commensurate with clinical colleagues in accordance with Agenda for Change (Band 5 upwards).
- Service Level Agreement specifying type of service, clinical specification (time-limited, maximum number of sessions, patient age, e.g., over eighteen years), personnel, costs, development strategy,
- Referral and assessment protocols for both short and longer term work.*

- Record keeping protocols.*
- Waiting list management protocol, including waiting list letters, feedback to GPs on waiting times etc.* See Authors' tip p.109.
- Quiet, safe, tidy rooms available for each counselling practitioner, preferably within general practice. Alternatives can be found if they suit local conditions.*
- Suitable chairs, desk, access to computer – realistic facilities for safe and respected work.*
- Practice leaflet on counselling service.*
- Access to counselling service protocol to include opt-in letters and times of service availability.*
- Administration of letters, working procedures; e.g., appointment bookings.
- Time: clinical and administrative (CPC recommend a ration of 60:40 clinical to administrative).
- Clinical supervision (CPC recommend a minimum of 1.5 hours a month individual supervision for every counsellor).*
- Grievance and disciplinary procedure.
- Time and setting for clinical liaison and collaboration within the primary care team and within the counselling service.
- Audit, clinical and service evaluation procedures.
- Liaison and collaboration routes and opportunities, both formal and informal.
- Training and personal development plans.
- Appraisals linked to training.
- Support – management, professional, personal

---

* Denotes inclusion in CPC Guidelines and Protocols (CPC, 2004).

METHOD

- Apportion resources according to budget and appropriate terms and conditions.
- Appoint counsellors according to person specification.
- Interview rigorously according to criteria. It is essential to have a panel for this part of the procedure – these can be found at local practices, Human Resources Departments and PCTs.
- Mix well – counsellors of all modalities are found to be suited to this recipe. Appoint clinical supervisors according to clinical criteria.
- Set contractual terms for supervisors according to pay scales.
- Design and produce all necessary clinical protocols and disseminate widely. These are best produced in collaboration with other mental health services. Leave to stand for some time to allow for working alliances to be established – it is useful to check on progress frequently, particularly in the early stages.
- Remove from heat periodically and review consistency.
- Intervene as necessary.
- Maintain close liaison with all counsellors through regular meetings, workshops, and training days.
- Maintain high-profile attendance at mental health strategy meetings at local and national levels.
- Establish, maintain, and make use of relationships at all levels.

Note: This dish can be enjoyed immediately and over time. It improves greatly with age but needs constant attention. Quantities can be increased in relation to patient numbers but also in relation to deprivation and need indicators.

Authors' tip

A recent research study on patients who did not attend for appointments revealed the importance of collaboration between counsellors and referring GPs (Snape, Perren, Jones, & Rowland, 2003). The research showed that the reasons for non-attendance were varied, but revealed that the manner in which the GP conducted the initial consultation, together with how long was the intervening waiting period from referral to first counselling appointment, were major factors in take-up. As a result of the research the team implemented some simple changes to their referral practice:

- patients are no longer referred urgently;
- patients are no longer referred at first consultation;
- people are encouraged to continue to see the GP while waiting for counselling;
- waiting list letters are sent after all referrals giving details of waiting time;
- counsellors give regular information to GPs about waiting times in order to help GPs decide when and whether to refer.

And what of Alison, Karen and Barbara?

We were dreading setting up a managed service in the PCT. We had been used to years of independent contracting under fund holding. But after following your recipe for Primary Care Surprise we couldn't believe how simple it was. Now we have best counselling practice on a daily basis, all within a modern NHS framework. Our health professional colleagues love our service and can't get enough of it . . . we wish we had followed your recipe earlier . . .! Thank you ,Wonder Counsellor Woman!

And Dr Stephen?

Hmm, when I heard what they were cooking up I must admit I was a bit sceptical. . . . Couldn't see why we had to change anything really when it had all been running fine the way we were . . . still, seems to be working well now and things seem more efficient. With the waiting list management, the referral protocols, and our regular clinical meetings I know much more about which patients would best be helped by the counselling available in the surgery. Our DNA rate seems to have gone down too, which is very good news, and the patients who are receiving counselling are clearly benefiting . . . we can see this easily from the CORE data that is coming out . . . they all seem very pleased with the service . . .

Well, a girl can dream can't she?!

And finally . . .

It is essential that counselling is given a professional basis in the NHS. As we write the auspices for this are good. Agenda for Change offers the first real possibility of terms and conditions for counsellors and psychotherapists that are commensurate with other health professionals on equivalent job evaluations. It also offers the possibility of a career trajectory for counsellors within the NHS organization. Statutory regulation beckons, indications are that the DoH would like to see this by 2008. This will bring with it certain requirements and, in our opinion, welcome standards of training and placement programmes for the professional counsellor.

For those who are already committed to professional standards and regulation, through their own ethical practice and those of their professional body, this will cause no real difficulties and will secure for them the protection of their title and their profession. It will also be a move forward in securing respect and authority for the profession in the eyes of our other health professionals, colleagues, and the public. For others who may be less well trained it will provide an opportunity for further training, CPD, and personal therapy to ensure best, safe, and useful practice

For those of you who are involved in setting up psychological services in advance of regulation it is wise to be aware of the aims of regulation in the future, and be part of this process of regulation, job evaluation, and professionalization.

It's easy – the ten-step programme for a clinical service manager

1. Make your case in accordance with government policy – clinical governance; treatment guidance; evidence based practice.
2. Select and recruit according to person specification.
3. Cut your cloth to fit the budget – plan for development and training.
4. Make it real – say what can be done by whom and with what resources.
5. Demonstrate it – use regular audits and evaluation and keep abreast of research. Undertake research within your service.

6. Make it safe – clear boundaries; safe practitioners; confidentiality; and collaboration clarity.
7. Make it ethical and legal and operate with probity.
8. Liase and collaborate – your colleagues are your allies.
9. Keep abreast of policy developments – put yourself about!
10. Enjoy your work and your colleagues.

CHAPTER SIX

TRAINING AND DEVELOPMENT

Outlines and aims

Counselling is a distinct profession. This chapter provides an outline of the necessary training for the professional NHS counsellor. It gives details on the components and competencies required, the requirements for clinical placements, the distinctions of management, mentoring, and supervision and how to implement and maintain continuing professional development for counsellors and managers.

* * * * *

What's in a name?

Counsellor, psychotherapist, psychoanalyst, psychologist, psychiatrist, psychiatric nurse – with all these names you might be forgiven for being somewhat confused and even sceptical about who does what and why. Such a plethora of titles doesn't exactly inspire confidence! But there is method in our madness – these titles do hold differences – and it is possible to see your way through the professional maze and to get some clarity. It is our aim to pave the way in this chapter, although in so doing we are bound to step on some toes.

Counselling, psychotherapy, and counselling psychology are all professions of psychological therapy in their own right and there is considerable overlap between them. Psychiatry and psychiatric nursing are medical professions and not the same as therapeutic professions. As such, alongside GPs, they are close working colleagues of the psychotherapeutic therapist but trained very differently to work with mental illness inside the medical profession. Thus, it is not in the scope of this book to consider the related medical professions further, other than in their roles as valued colleagues and experienced clinicians.

In the world of counselling in primary care you will find clinicians in all three categories of counselling, psychotherapy, and psychology. Within the next ten years it is highly likely, if not certain, that the terms will be restricted for use; in other words, statutorily regulated by those who have undergone an agreed training programme. It may be that there will be but one professional title; for example, psychological therapist. Meanwhile, the professional bodies set their own codes of ethics practice, training standards, and requirements for continuing the professional body against which professional counsellors can be recruited.

While the fine detail for statutory regulation is still to be debated and agreed, the picture is not as confused or as unregulated as some might fear. For the commissioning NHS Trust and newly appointed counselling service manager the process of recruitment to counselling posts can be fairly straightforward as long as you recruit counsellors against agreed training and qualification criteria in terms of:

- professional training – which includes theory, experiential work, personal therapy, and supervised clinical practice;
- clinical placement;
- knowledge of specialist NHS areas;
- membership of professional body/codes of ethical practice;
- Ongoing clinical supervision.

The most important message is that counselling is a distinct profession – it is not something you tack on to another job, that you know how to do because you are a good listener, or something that you can learn on a weekend workshop. Like medicine or engineering it takes years of training, personal investment, and development. And just like medicine or engineering it is important that the professional counsellor has undergone a process of learning and achieved recognition by a formal body set up for this purpose. This may not be an absolute guarantee of competence, but it is generally accepted, as in all other professions, to be an indication. Without it there are no indicators.

Agreeing to disagree

What is encouraging in the relatively new profession of counselling is that setting standards of selection, training, and definitions of qualifying processes are taken very seriously by all the main bodies. As such there is considerable agreement and, of course, some disagreement. It is hard to state categorically exactly the body of knowledge to be learnt and how to practise definitively. Counselling and psychotherapy is relationship based, perhaps more than any other profession. It is not a medical profession, although some nurses and doctors do go on to train as counsellors and psychotherapists.

You could say it is closer to parenting than it is to doctoring or engineering. As such the body of knowledge, characteristics, personal attributes, and personal insight required are even harder to agree on, to select for, and then to evaluate. But most would agree this uncertainty is no reason not to try to set standards that can be agreed amongst the profession.

This is helpful to employers, particularly the NHS, and to patients, and to would-be counsellors. It is also helpful in that it establishes that the work involved in the understanding of the human condition, and the difficulties we can all get into, is serious, complex and takes a great deal of hard work to manage.

The transformation of emotional and psychological pain into illness, the presentation of psychological distress, the array of different aspects of mental illness, are responsible for a vast amount of the work done in the NHS, primarily in primary care. GPs, counsellors and psychotherapists who are properly trained to work in this field know this, and know how to bring about effective change. Thus, in fiscal terms alone, getting the treatment of mental health problems in primary care more right than wrong is a serious business for the NHS. At the moment far too much is spent on quick-fix prescribing and scatter-shot referring, much of which is lost in non-compliance and escalation of the problems rather than on thoughtful, timely, therapeutic interventions. '30–60% of patients do not take their medication as prescribed and the many reasons for this include drug factors such as side effects and also health beliefs and behaviours of patients and prescribers' (Mendlewicz, 2001). Both the NHS and the counselling and psychotherapy professions therefore have a duty to set rigorous standards and codes of practice in order the get best practice overall .

Who are these guys?

The main professional bodies, all of whom set and maintain criteria, are :

- The Association of Counsellors and Psychotherapists in primary care (CPC);
- The United Kingdom Council for Psychotherapy (UKCP);
- The British Association for Counselling and Psychotherapy (BACP);
- The British Psychological Society (BPS).

As stated in Chapter Five, the Counselling and Psychotherapy Forum for Primary Care has brought together these various bodies to establish agreed minimum training standards for counsellors working in the NHS. These are linked to the Band 5 person specification given in Appendix 1. Note that this is a minimum standard and many counsellors, and particularly psychotherapists, are trained to a much higher initial standard and greater depth than this minimum.

Utopia

If we were starting from scratch, right now, we might establish a much simpler and more uniform national training standard. If we ruled the world the training of counsellors would be like that of, say, teacher training. In this ideal world you could go anywhere in the country, undertake a post-graduate counselling training and know that it would fit the bill. You might undertake a psychodynamic counselling training which would be different in content to, say, a gestalt training, but they will both be to *the same standard*, just as the geography teacher is trained to the same standard and rigour as her colleague in the French department.

Meanwhile, back in the real world, though the picture can be confusing, the regulation of the field by the professional bodies is helping. This in turn is resulting in most training bodies setting their selection criteria, training content, and clinical practice in accordance with these expectations. It is hoped we will continue to see a withering away of trainings that offer a 'boil in the bag' approach to counselling training.

Of the bodies listed above, CPC has set a specific training standard with which members have to accord, although they acknowledge various routes to achieve this. The UKCP works on a sectional basis, and the various sections set their own criteria to which their organizational members concur. The BACP has different categories of membership and only those who are accredited have to achieve certain criteria. However non-accredited members may well have met this standard but chosen not to seek accreditation. The British Psychological Society operates differently again, and clinical psychologists follow a specific post-graduate degree route to chartered clinical psychology/counselling psychology.

Note that clinical psychologists are not necessarily trained in either psychodynamic or humanistic counselling or psychotherapy, but are trained in clinical psychology, which includes cognitive–behavioural therapy and other similar therapeutic approaches. However, chartered counselling psychologists have undergone specific therapeutic training after their initial psychology degree. Psychology posts within the NHS already use agreed person specifications and grading scales in accordance with BPS structure. This is not yet the case for counselling or adult psychotherapy posts.

So that's all clear isn't it!

The professional counsellor

If you were advertising and interviewing for counsellors for a new primary care counselling service designed to meet the needs of Central Anywhere PCT, how would you describe the person(s) sought? Here are few very varied versions – all based on real examples.

Spot the difference

Wanted: counsellors for primary care counselling service provided within the Mental Health Trust. Applicants should be trained counsellors or show an interest in a variety of counselling approaches. Previous work experience in an NHS setting and a nursing or related professional background would be desirable. Knowledge of mental heath essential.

Comment: This specification is not sufficient since it neither specifies training as essential nor does it specify what training level or qualification is required, leaving itself wide open to applicants with no formal training at all. Would you advertise a post for GP specifying an interest in medicine as an alternative to full training? Also, there is no reason why nursing is a desirable background – counsellors and psychotherapists come from a variety of backgrounds and usually enter training at a later life stage. Knowledge of NHS mental health policy, organizational structure would be advantageous, and is now covered in specific post-graduate NHS specific modules.

Applicants are sought from suitably qualified and experienced counsellors for the post of primary care counsellor. Candidates will need to be able to assess and work with a wide range of mental health referrals. Essential qualifications : BACP accreditation; completion of a BACP accredited course or equivalent.

Comment: better, but not clear enough. BACP accreditation is an excellent standard but it is not the same as completion of a BACP accredited course, since accreditation requires completion of 450 clinical hours in addition to core training. Also, this excludes candidates who have done a perfectly good training on a non-BACP accredited course and the necessary counselling hours. However, this might be covered by the word equivalent, in which case the BACP accreditation statement is irrelevant. Better to phrase it in terms of a specified training standard and say that this includes BACP accreditation/CPC Registration/ UKCP registered psychotherapist/BPS Charter.

We are seeking to recruit experienced counsellors to work in our primary care counselling service. Candidates must be trained to a minimum of post-graduate diploma level in counselling or psychotherapy. They should have a minimum of 100 hours post-qualification experience in an NHS or equivalent placement, and have undertaken NHS specific modules in their initial training or subsequently. They should have at least two years' clinical experience in another setting. Candidates who are CPC registered/BACP accredited/UKCP registered psychotherapists/BPS chartered counselling psychologists will meet the training criteria specified.

Comment: Bingo! Here the generic training criteria comes first, then the clinical post-qualification placement experience plus further training for NHS specific work, and finally the necessary clinical experience. The various professional bodies are then listed as equivalent, but none of them is specified as the particular benchmark.

Minimum training criteria

So, we can sum up the minimum training and qualification criteria for a primary counsellor as:

- postgraduate diploma level counselling or psychotherapy;
- core theoretical model – this could be specific, e.g., psychodynamic or integrative but must be coherent;
- minimum of 450 hours of skills and theory content in training;
- minimum 100 hours' clinical placement while training;
- At least forty hours' personal therapy;
- post-qualification 100 hours' placement in NHS – like a GP registrar;
- clinical experience in other settings;
- membership of stated professional body and adherence to codes of practice (CPC/BACP/UKCP/BPS).

If you are recruiting for senior posts, managers, supervisors, etc., then clearly you will need to state the additional training, qualifications, CPD, and clinical experience required accordingly. The above is the bedrock for the professional counsellor career trajectory in the NHS. Everything should follow from this.

Authors' tip

When on selection panels, either as an external adviser to selecting prospective trainees for counselling trainings or selecting from qualified counsellors for clinical placements or posts in primary care, you need to follow procedure that allows equal access to all. So questions should be fair and equal for all candidates. However, we have found it useful to also bear in mind an inner set of questions – 'In due course would I refer a patient to this person?'; if the selection is for NHS work, 'Could I see them working well in a primary care team?'; and finally, 'Would I like to work with them as a colleague?'

Education, education, education!

So why are all these elements in the training of counsellors so important?

Linda, our PCT primary care development manager, has been charged, together with Alison, the newly appointed counselling manager, with restructuring and recruiting for the new counselling service. She is puzzled by all the varying definitions she hears about counselling. Surely it is just a question of being professional and knowing how to listen? You can hear her well-intentioned scepticism echoing the halls of PCTs.

Alison tries to break down all the components to explain why this degree of training is so essential and how important each component is and how this differentiates the competency and the work of the trained psychological therapist.

Selection – what makes a good counsellor

The first thing to emphasize is that counselling is both an education – there is a body of knowledge to learn – and a training – you also find out how to be a practitioner. So, when taking on trainee counsellors, training institutes need to be looking for people who can manage both. The other thing to note is that those who are damaged or disturbed themselves often seek training in order to feel better; to indirectly get the help they need, or to mask their difficulties. This makes the process of selection even trickier in this field and, I would suggest, in most of the so-called 'caring professions'. Academic selection criteria, while useful, are only part of the story – what is needed on any counselling training is strict clinical criteria too. Ideally applicants should:

- meet certain academic standards (initial degree or equivalent professional qualification);
- undergo a personal individual interview which has components of health scrutiny and psychological assessment;
- take part in a group process to see how they work with others.

This is essential and can help enormously in preventing people who are in need of help themselves in becoming misdirected into training.

A theoretical model –
the professional core

Counselling bodies require at least 450 hours of theory and skills learning and training on a post graduate diploma level course. This sets both *the standard and depth* of learning (post graduate diploma) and the *duration* (450 hours over, optimally, upwards of three years). This recognizes the maturity, the academic ability, and the personal robustness required for the work. The best courses take place over a lengthy period of time with plenty of tutor/ supervisor/trainer contact and personal therapy. This time element allows for:

- important personal insight to develop;
- continual appraisal and support for all;
- comprehensive coverage of theory and skills;
- the opportunity for students who find they cannot manage what is required to end their training at any time in such a way that they are supported;
- mature students to undertake training alongside a part-time job or personal responsibilities.

The theory covered will vary depending on the model of training that the counsellor has undertaken. Where once there was Freud and psychoanalysis there are now many different counselling and psychotherapeutic theories, variations on which proliferate still. The range of 'brand names' can be very confusing. The distinction between counselling and psychotherapy is blurred, too. As we have seen, many counsellors in primary care are qualified psychotherapists.

However, it is beyond the scope of this book to try to define even some of the main brands of psychotherapy and counselling models, let alone list the many other outlying varieties. Suffice to say that today there is no one single dominant theoretical approach in counselling services in the NHS. But we can suggest that there is considerable overlap and similarity in method and approach, particularly in respect to the relational aspects of the work, namely the transference, and to the understanding of unconscious processes. Each approach brings a perspective to ideas about psychopathology, personality, assessment, treatment, and interventions. The exception to this might be cognitive–behavioural therapy.

The Department of Health Guideline: *Treatment Choice in Psychological Therapies and Counselling* (DoH, 2001) defines counselling in the NHS thus :

> Counselling is a systematic process which gives individuals an opportunity to explore, discover and clarify ways of living more resourcefully, with a greater sense of well being. Counselling may be concerned with addressing and resolving specific problems, making decisions, coping with crises, working through conflict or improving relationships with others. Counsellors may practise within any of the therapeutic approaches: psychodynamic counselling, cognitive behavioural counselling, systemic counselling and so on . . . the work of most counsellors is generalist (analogous to general practice) and is not necessarily linked to diagnostic categories . . .

This is a good definition, but we would add that although the work may not be linked to diagnostic categories it is linked to assessment and treatment formulation. Thus, the counsellor can be relied upon to know what is best in the context of the treatment options available. Also, there is no inclusion in the above definition of clinical improvement. CORE data from counselling services around the country clearly shows that, as well as all of the above aims, counselling also produces significant clinical change.

So, in the context of primary care we would stress that a counsellor needs a thorough bedrock of theory to make sense of what she works with, i.e., the human condition in all its manifestations. However, we would also stress that no one theoretical approach has ascendancy in terms of being better suited to primary care work . . . the counsellor also needs extensive training in skills in order to assess, contain, hold, and think about the many uncertainties aroused in a confused, unstable, ill, and damaged patient. The trained counsellor and psychotherapist has all these attributes and thus is a very safe and useful pair of hands. The majority of primary care counsellors are sufficiently trained practitioners and their value is irreplaceable in the NHS. No other profession has this particular approach and understanding of health, mental and physical.

The sort of theory covered in a good enough post graduate level counselling diploma training will be along the following lines.

- An understanding of models of the psyche/mind – e.g., the unconscious, the defences, the ego states, personality types (this will vary according to the main model), which will include comprehensive coverage of leading thinkers, e.g., Freud, Jung, Rogers, Klein, Winnicott, Perle, Bion, Bowlby, Kohut, etc.
- An understanding of human development from birth to adulthood.

- A good knowledge of the range of counselling and psychotherapeutic models.
- Family systems.
- Group dynamics.
- Psychopathology.
- Clinical concepts and techniques.
- Introductory psychiatry – knowledge of mental illness and mental health.
- Cross-cultural issues.
- Ontology.
- Ethics and the law.
- Research knowledge and methods.
- Evaluation, audit and outcome.

Trainees are continually and summarily assessed, both academically, through written work, and clinically through experiential group work and supervised client work, in all these areas of study.

NHS specific training

Several course now run, or have run, specific health care/NHS/primary care modules that trainees can take either as part of their initial diploma or as additional modules following qualification in generic counselling/psychotherapy. We hope that training institutes will develop some conformity in this regard and offer post-qualification options for counsellors wishing to graduate with an NHS specialism. This would be linked to a suitable clinical placement (see below) and to national accreditation within the NHS.

Meanwhile, most counsellors achieve coverage of further theoretical and organizational aspects necessary for work in an NHS setting either through work covered in their initial diploma training, a post-qualification placement in primary care (see below), a range of CPD; and/or learning on the hoof. For many it has been a combination of all of these – quite evolutionary, in fact.

Broadly speaking we would see the content of such a specialist module to include detailed coverage of the following areas:

- NHS structure and policy;
- clinical governance;
- NHS multi-disciplinary working;
- knowledge of NHS mental health policy, strategy, and procedures;
- psychotropic medicine;
- medical diagnoses of mental illness (*Diagnostic and Statistical Manual [DSM]*);
- risk assessment and referral pathways;
- audit, evaluation and outcome measurement;
- research methods and content;
- notes and record-keeping;
- confidentiality, collaboration, and the law;
- psychiatric placement;
- the philosophy of medicine.

This would be acquired through taught content and clinical experience and validated through the awarding body of the training institute.

Meanwhile, as we write, most counsellors achieve coverage of these further theoretical and organisational aspects necessary for work in an NHS setting either:

- through work covered in their initial diploma training;

- through a post-qualification placement in primary care (see below);
- through a range of CPD;
- through learning on the hoof.

In reality, most experienced counsellors now employed in the NHS have achieved their expertise through a combination of all of these factors. The arrival at the profession of NHS psychological therapist has been, and still is, quite an evolutionary process. It is very much work in progress.

Clinical placements

The clinical placement is an essential part of counselling or psychotherapy training. This is how you find out whether you can work with people effectively and help bring about useful psychological change. Having the theoretical knowledge is one thing but being able to work with real people, in all sorts of confusion, distress, rage, and despair is another. Training involves a long-term commitment to developing these skills through rigorous supervision of properly chosen training clients. Such clients should be assessed by experienced clinicians and only given as training clients if suitable. The supervision provided must fit with the training model and close contact between tutors, supervisors, and placement mangers maintained throughout.

We would offer the following guidance on training placements.

- All placements, if not in house, should be vetted by the training course managers. Students should not be left wandering around the locality trying to find somewhere they can acquire the necessary training hours.

- Close collaboration should be established and maintained between the course, the supervisor(s), and the placement.
- Counsellors are supervised, in house, by experienced supervisors for a minimum of 1.5 hours of group supervision a week.
- Supervisors have a significant input into trainee appraisal.
- All clients are assessed by experienced counsellors before being allocated to trainees.
- Trainees undertake a minimum of 100 hours clinical placement experience throughout their training and considerably more than this is desirable.
- A general practice setting is not a suitable place for a trainee placement unless the student is in his or her final year or post-qualification. If students are in placement in primary care, then this has to be part of a managed counselling scheme with appropriate supervision and under the mentorship of an experienced in-house practice counsellor who undertakes assessments.

NHS post-qualification placements

In addition to the clinical hours undertaken as part of initial core training, CPC recommends that graduates wishing to work in the NHS undertake a post-qualification placement or training period in an NHS setting. This is viewed as similar to the period of work of a GP registrar or assistant psychology post, set up to gain further experience, understanding, and knowledge of the NHS setting and the wider range of presenting problems. In particular, newly qualified counsellors will learn models of collaboration, team working, legal and ethical requirements specific to statutory work in the NHS. They will also become familiar with the degree of complexity and severity in primary care work. Again this should be under the guidance of an experienced in-house counsellor or psychotherapist who acts as mentor and teacher and provides personal support. Clinical supervision is provided elsewhere alongside the mentoring.

Authors' tip

This model has been used with great success in large managed counselling services throughout the country (Derbyshire, Sheffield, Newcastle, Darlington, etc.) as an ideal way to offer the necessary post-qualification training needed for NHS work. Managed Counselling Schemes such as that in Southern Derbyshire have developed their own syllabus and attainment principals for counsellors in placement, covering many of the areas outlined above.

Newly qualified and experienced counsellors with no previous experience in primary care are interviewed and selected for their potential to work in the setting. They are then offered a placement within a training practice under the mentorship of the practice counsellor. The placement is for a minimum of six months and may well take longer, depending on the skill and experience of the new counsellor. The mentor and NQC (newly qualified counsellor) meet on a weekly basis and work through the content as well as monitoring the management of the clinical work. The NQC takes on a maximum of four clients a week, all of which are assessed for suitability by the mentor counsellor. The aim is also to work towards undertaking assessment towards the end of the placement. Supervision is provided separately.

> Having completed the placement, counsellors are then appraised and validated as experienced and qualified in all aspects of NHS counselling work.
>
> In many regards this is akin to the initial post-training year for a newly qualified teacher, a GP registrar, or an assistant psychologist.

Supervision

One of the essential bedrocks of counselling training and ongoing work is clinical supervision. It is hard to describe what this is, though there are many things *it is not*, namely management, training, teaching, or leadership. However, paradoxically it does include many of these aspects. But over and above all this, clinical supervision is essentially about the processing of psychological dynamic intrapsychic and interpsychic material. Since this is the diagnostic and the raw and transformational material for all psychological therapeutic work then, *q.e.d*, supervision is essential.

Supervision is variously defined thus:

A quintessential interpersonal interaction with the general goal that one person, the supervisor, meets with another in an effort to make the latter more effective in helping people. [Hess, 1980]

An intensive, interpersonally focused, one-to-one relationship in which one person is designated to facilitate the development of therapeutic competence in another person. [Loganbill, Hardy, & Delworth, 1982]

An arrangement between two qualified persons where one offers to help the other reflect on his/her counselling work and the context surrounding it. [Caroll, 1996]

The key words in all these definitions are:

- interpersonal;
- relationship;
- intensive;
- help;
- reflect;
- contextual;

but further to this supervision has an even wider remit, particularly in primary care, it can be said to be:

- educative, supportive and managerial (Hawkins & Shohut, 1989);
- and formative, restorative and normative (Proctor, undated).

In their model of clinical supervision in primary care, Butterton and Murphy (2002) describe the particular context of primary care and outline a model of supervision that considers the psychological processes of the work context. This model is specific to the needs of the newly qualified primary care counsellor. Here the role of the mentor (see above) is structured in relation to that of the supervisor, so that the management of the client by the counsellor in the context of the primary care team is attended to by the mentor and the intra and interpsychological processes are attended to by the supervisor. Once the counsellor has completed her placement she will 'let go' of her mentor and retain the management and observance of contextual matters herself. Meanwhile, the role of clinical supervision continues.

So supervision is a must for all counsellors as long as they continue to practise – it becomes a regular part of your daily clinical work, like personal hygiene in relation to your daily life. Personally, we would no more do without regular supervision than we would regular baths. All the professional bodies stipulate that supervision is a requirement of ethical practice.

The supervisor, the manager, and the counsellor

The supervisor

When you are an experienced clinician you use your own judgement and contacts to find a supervisor who is a good fit for you. Like repainting the bedroom it's good to have a change once in a while too, as this gives you a fresh eye and stops the possibility of collusion in any areas. The minimum requirement for ongoing post-qualification supervision is 1.5 hours a month individual or equivalent.

CPC provides a list of registered supervisors for primary care and NHS counsellors for which they have set an agreed training and qualification standard. This includes the stipulation that supervisors of primary care counsellors have themselves worked in primary care or the NHS and have considerable clinical experience of these settings. (See CPC *Guidelines and Protocols*, 2004.) In managed services the supervisors may well be appointed directly by the service. Alternatively, they will be selected and contracted by the individual counsellor. This will depend on the model of the service (see below). Either way it is essential that the supervisor is competent to work with a primary care model.

The manager

Like the clinical supervisor, the manager of an NHS counselling service needs specific and specialist training and experience over and above that of her clinical training. She also needs directorial support and a coherent organizational structure to support her and her service. At present there are no formal management trainings for counselling service managers, but individual clinical managers can attain the necessary training in a number of ways:

- previous transferable managerial experience/training in other professions;
- in-house shadowing programmes;
- in-house training (at Trust level or at Strategic Regional Authority level);
- NHS management programmes, e.g., Kings Fund;
- fully directed and supported on-the-job experience – useful personal appraisal programmes tied to training needs;
- individual consultation;
- trainee management pilots.

However, in these early days we look forward to more integration of clinical counselling service managers into the organizational and training structures of the NHS. It is essential that their training needs are identified and seen as equivalent to those of other high level NHS management and leadership staff.

Authors' tip

Since the role of the clinical service manager is even more recent than that of the professional counsellor, most existing service managers have learnt the role on the hoof, so to speak. Many have brought with them management experience from previous professions and disciplines such as teaching, commerce, etc. In Newcastle an innovative project has been piloted to enable counsellors interested in clinical service management to shadow the existing clinical service manager as a trainee clinical manager. For a six-month period the trainee shadowed the manager in all aspects of her work for a designated part of the working week. The project was flexible enough to allow the trainee to get a flavour of most aspects of the post over the project's duration. She also took on specific ring-fenced projects and attended meetings, and had training in specific aspects of the post, e.g., budgeting/employment issues, etc. For further information see *CPC Review* (2004).

Making connections

In an NHS managed counselling service it is important that the manager has a formal relationship with supervisors of the counsellors working in the service. As we have seen, the context of primary care is complex and the organizational dynamics of the team provide fertile ground for psychological conundrums. So the supervisor has a crucial role in helping the counsellor understand this and keep her eye on the patient's concerns. The manager has an equally important role in providing professional support, employment support, and leadership. Proper, professional, accountable liaison between the manager and the supervisor helps this process and allows for clear discussion and help for the counsellor. It helps the counsellor to be clear about what support she is getting from whom and maintains clear boundaries between the two important functions of supervision and management.

The relationship between managed service and supervisor could take one of the following forms depending on how the service is structured in relation to the commissioning Trust (see Chapters Four and Five).

- The supervisor is employed within the scheme and is paid and contracted by the service to provide supervision to all employed counsellors. Clearly, in a large scheme there will be several supervisors more than likely providing group supervision.
- Individual counsellors establish their own supervision but the supervisors conform to an agreed standard. The supervisor has some kind of link, e.g., an annual report or regular meetings with the counselling service manager.
- The managed service is an out-of-house provider, e.g., Acme Shire Counselling Service, and provides supervision within its own organizational structure.

In this way matters of accountability are made clear and distinct. Also, any issues arising in respect of counsellor competency/counsellor/client safety can ideally be attended to before work breaks down in some way. The NHS counsellor should have nothing but help from her supervisor and her manager, and should not fear the loss of control or creativity in her practice by such arrangements being in place. On the contrary, it is the view of these authors that you should make use of all the help you can have – you're going to need it! However, this model does stipulate the need for the service manager to be clinically trained and to maintain a clinical practice. Otherwise the issues presented are not always understood psychologically, which can give rise to problems.

Training supervision

When in a training, as opposed to a post-qualification placement, there are certain additional aspects that supervision needs to provide. This reinforces the need for a formal relationship between supervisor and training provider. Supervisors on training courses should be contracted by the training organization and be included as part of the ongoing appraisal of students. Again, they need to meet the professional specification for supervisors, be trained, and have considerable clinical experience.

It is likely that there is a much a higher degree of the educative element in clinical supervision for trainees as well as considerable personal support. The training supervisor is attending to the trainee's capacity to develop. Sometimes at this stage there is an overlap between supervision and personal therapy. A good supervisor can often be the best person to help identify if certain problems in the work are arising due to difficulties within the therapist herself, as opposed to the client or the training. This takes us neatly to the next major element of training, which is that of personal therapy.

Personal therapy

This is one of the most hotly debated areas of training for counsellors and psychotherapists. The questions raised within the profession are:

- should personal therapy be mandatory?
- if so how much? Is this simply training therapy or thereafter?
- what should be the frequency?
- what type of therapy?

Once again the main professional bodies have more or less agreed on this and have stipulated a minimum. For example, CPC sets personal therapy as a required part of training and sets the minimum at forty hours. BACP is bit more open in its interpretation and recommends therapy, but also allows for experiential group work to be equivalent. The UKCP relies on its sections to set their requirements and, although most of these do stipulate personal therapy as a training requirement, notably one or two sections do not. For example, cognitive–behavioural therapists are not required to have personal therapy as part of their training and neither are family systemic therapists. Thus, some of the differences of opinion are related to differences in theoretical approach.

Before we move on perhaps it is worth emphasizing why the authors regard personal therapy as such an important part of our training and why, for example, CPC makes it a requirement for counsellors in primary care.

- Counselling is viewed as a process in which the client presents very subtle and deeply hidden, often unconscious clues as to his/her internal struggles/conflicts. These may manifest as symptoms, or behaviours, or emotions. The counsellor has to be very sure of his/her own self in order not to get lost or caught up in the patient's world and end up colluding or becoming distracted. In order to know what is going on in someone else you have to have a fair idea of where you are, of the boundary between you and the other person.

- A fundamental tenet of counselling is that it is more helpful to be responsible for your own life than not, to be emotionally self-autonomous. This must first apply to the counsellor.

- The dynamic nature of counselling, the interpersonal nature of the work, calls on all aspects of the counsellor's personality. What goes on in the therapeutic relationship is the nub of the work and it keeps changing. This means the counsellor must be vigilant and be able to self-reflect all the time to guard against 'unexamined parts of the self' getting in the way of what the client needs. It is like avoiding contaminating the patient, just as a nurse or doctor will try to avoid contaminating a patient with bacteria. Without your own therapy there is a danger you may be working your own difficulties out in relation to your patients.

- Often we are drawn to work as therapists because things have gone wrong in our own lives, often our early lives. This is no reason not to be a therapist but it does have to be worked out to a fair degree first. This is why therapy undertaken during training is so useful. Personally, we favour entering therapy before training

even begins, so you can discover whether it is therapeutic help you yourself need, or training, or both!

- The process of examining your own self and internal
world in the presence of another is unique and particular. Counsellors need to understand what is required
for this before they ask for it of others.
- Finally, it is a matter of professional interest, personal
safety and vitality that the counsellor undertakes therapy.

Of course, no one can be completely analysed, but in
the opinion of these authors you cannot be a good therapist without enough personal therapy. This is a view that is
reinforced the more we work and the more counsellors and
psychotherapists we work with, and it is a view we hold to
whether or not there is research to support it. Indeed, it is
a moot point as to whether the professional bodies are
right to suggest a minimum length of therapy at all. The
most important point, that *therapists should undertake*
enough *therapy in order that they can work at their best*, gets
lost in a discussion about numbers. For many counsellors
and psychotherapists this can mean upwards of several
years of once or twice or thrice weekly therapy.

Continuing professional development

Just as with supervision, so training continues long after
initial qualification. Once again, most of the professional
bodies are in agreement about the need and the quality of
CPD for professional counsellors and in particular those
working in the NHS.

All the professional bodies specify a yearly CPD
requirement for continuation of membership. This ranges

from 25–30 hours minimum and covers the following areas:

- training – workshops, seminars, etc.;
- attendance at conferences;
- formal networking;
- peer groups;
- professional writing;
- professional committee work;
- speaking, lecturing.

Every year there is a plethora of training days and conferences advertised, many of which are of a very high standard. Some are specific to the needs of NHS counsellors.

It is useful if the counselling service manager can keep abreast of what is available, both locally and nationally in order to help identify and manage the training needs of her staff. It is also essential to ensure that a training budget is allocated and reviewed annually. Individual appraisals with each counsellor will ensure that each person's training needs are identified and followed up (see Chapter Five).

Setting up bespoke training days by bringing trainers to your service and offering the training to all your counsellors in-house can be a very cheap and easily accessible way of providing necessary CPD to staff. It may be that colleagues within the NHS Trust can provide the training at little or no extra cost. If external trainers are needed, then such a trainer can be asked to design a day specifically catering to your group of staff. This also a good way of ensuring that your counsellors training needs are attended to and that they receive support and acknowledgement for this important area.

Summary

So now you know how to recognize a professional counsellor and how to select one for your service. Whether you are a manager, a trust commissioner, a GP, or a would-be counsellor, we hope this chapter has helped you understand what is needed for the work of a psychotherapeutic counsellor and why and how to go about getting the necessary training and resources.

. . . Ten steps to heaven !

To be a professional counsellor in the NHS you need:

- a minimum core training to postgraduate diploma level in counselling or psychotherapy or a charter in counselling psychology (at least 450 hours of taught theory and skills);
- further CPD/taught modules in NHS specific topics;
- a supervised clinical training placement (minimum 100 hours);
- a minimum of forty hours personal therapy but ideally much more;
- a clinical placement in an NHS setting or equivalent (e.g., non-statutory organization receiving referrals from the NHS);
- membership of a recognized professional body (CPC/BACP/UKCP/BPS) that has an agreed code of ethical practice;
- ongoing clinical supervision;
- ongoing continued professional development training (minimum of thirty hours a year);

- professional indemnity insurance;
- good sense of humour, skin like an elephant's hide, and a liking for uncomfortable chairs and endless Hob Nobs (or Rich Tea if you're in that sort of practice!).

ENJOY!

CHAPTER SEVEN

IMPLICATIONS OF THE MANAGED SERVICE MODEL

Outline and aims

The intention of this final chapter is to reflect on the virtues or otherwise of establishing managed counselling services within the NHS. We discuss the implications of such developments for the counselling profession, for other health and medical professions, for treatment approaches to mental health, and for the employment conditions of counsellors in the future.

*   *   *   *   *

Strange bedfellows

We have long since thought that marrying psychotherapeutic practice with medical practice is strange. It is not exactly doomed to fail, but it is fraught with fascinating tensions and complexities – many of which reflect our own individual psychological struggles and the wish for simple solutions as opposed to those which may require hard work and pain! You could say some of the tussles between the two orthodoxies are like those between our rational selves and our unconscious. However, all of us working in the health service are sharing in the same project: that of containing and alleviating the fears and pain of others. Sometimes this involves permanent change, often it involves acceptance and clarification of personal responsibility. Whether we are doctors or therapists we are wrestling with our own uncertainties and anxieties in dealing with that of others and we are often motivated to do this work for complex and hidden reasons. As Tom Main put it in his wonderful paper, written in 1957 but still utterly relevant to today's NHS:

> We know that doctors and nurses undertake the work of alleviating human suffering because of deep personal reasons, and that the practice of medicine like every human activity has abiding unconscious determinants. We also know that if human needs are not satisfied, they tend to become more passionate, to be reinforced by aggression and then to deteriorate in maturity, with sadism invading the situation . . . until ultimate despair can ensue. [Main, 1957]

Strange bedfellows we may well be, GPs and therapists, but important allies in the arena of mental health so that neither party vents their frustrations on the patients in the guise of treatment or on each other in the guise of championing one approach over the other.

Medical practice has long been based on an adherence to scientific verifiability and latterly is laced with protocols, evidence-based treatments, guidelines, diagnosis, measurement, appraisal, budget-driven economies in relation to prescribing and treatment options, etc. Most of this has evolved quite properly to safeguard the patient and the taxpayer (who are, in fact, one and the same). The patient is regarded as someone who comes to the doctor for something to be diagnosed and treated and cured. The doctor is 'in charge' of the patient. Yet everyone who works in medicine knows that it is rarely, if ever, as simple as this and no more so than in primary care.

John Launer, a very experienced GP who has worked alongside psychotherapists and counsellors in his team for many years and who advocates the use of clinical supervision for GPs as well as for therapists, describes primary care thus:

> Primary care, as a rule, is not characterised by the proverbial sore throats, dressings and in-growing toenails that the public may imagine, nor by the relatively trivial function of 'gate-keeping' as understood by many specialists and politicians. It is a place of refuge for those whose problems permanently defy definition or who are too disturbed or frightened to go anywhere else. [Burton & Launer, 2003]

Most GPs will instantly recognize Launer's description. It would follow from this that general practice is indeed the natural territory for the work of the professional psychological therapist. But more often the patient in general practice is regarded as someone who comes to the doctor for something to be diagnosed and treated and cured. The systems set up, and the consequent resourcing thereof, seem to assume that patients will neatly fit into simple categories of ailment or illness and that the GP, by following protocol (see for example the NICE guidelines), can bring about an expedient cure or amelioration. Yet everyone who works in medicine knows that it is rarely, if ever, as simple as this and no more so than in primary care – as Launer so graphically describes.

Counselling and psychotherapy, on the other hand, are based on the movement of the individual to self-knowledge

and autonomy and the medium for treatment is the therapeutic relationship. The principle responsibility for any
useful work lies with the individual. The territory for
change rests in the maze of the unconscious, which is
unpacked through the treatment process and through the
transference and countertransference experienced between
the patient and the therapist.

The two systems sound quite different even at this level
of simplification, and yet these professionals, GPs and
therapists, can work very closely together to best serve
thousands of people who present on a daily basis as
distressed, disturbed, ill, and confused.

Let us look at what has emerged as a result of bringing
these two strange bedfellows together over these last
decades – have we had creative intercourse and produced
healthy thriving babies, or has it been like the mating of
the horse and the donkey – producing an ass!

The practical

A simple, pragmatic, answer to what has emerged is that
there has definitely been a sea-change in the professionalism of counsellors and that this has developed as a result
of work in the NHS. As well as the work of the professional bodies, notably that of CPC and BACP, we also
have the NHS to thank for insisting on this. Where once
we had a loose band of unidentified individuals with no
particular accountability other than to their own codes of
ethics and possibly their GP partners, we now see established services with formal terms and conditions and the
respect, status, and efficiency that goes with this. Clinical
governance drove this with its insistence on equity,

accountability, best practice, and monitoring. While some counsellors might debate that these structures bring restrictions to their clinical freedom, most would agree that the lot of the primary care counsellor within a managed service is more secure, more professional, and more respected than ever before. Most would also agree that this improves the lot of the patient since they can access counselling more easily and certainly more equitably in areas where the services are adequately resourced and managed. Thankfully, this is gradually becoming the opinion of many health service managers and medical colleagues, many of whom see the muddle and confusion in relation to counsellors' conditions of employment, practice, and training as counterproductive to equity, good employment practice, good management and, most important of all, good clinical practice.

The Sainsbury Centre, in its independent policy review on the development of primary care mental health services (*Primary Solutions*, 2003), talks of the emergence of practice counsellors as having been 'one of the outstanding developments in primary care in recent years', and goes on to say

> . . . this development has been influenced by a number of factors, including a shift in emphasis in the work of CMHTs, the added flexibility given to practices by fund holding and a genuine concern among GPs to provide more effective care for service users whose problems result from chaotic life experience.

However, all is by no means rosy. The effective use of counselling and psychotherapy may well have been growing steadily in the NHS and in particular in primary care since the 1980s. The DoH commissioned *Treatment*

Choice in Psychological Therapies and Counselling: Evidence Based Clinical Practice Guideline (DoH, 2001) states quite clearly that 'Psychological therapy should be routinely considered as a treatment option when assessing mental health problems . . .'.

But if this is going to continue to be a real possibility for every patient who both needs and prefers this option, then we must have the right clinicians in place who can assess for this treatment option and provide it if it is considered appropriate and is in line with patient preference. However, even as we write there are large pockets of the country with no first line primary care psychological therapy service, still no statutory pay scales for counsellors in the NHS, and no clear agreement as to how counselling services should be structured or managed in order to best provide the possibility of good psychological treatment in primary care.

As we have learnt, a snapshot of counselling arrangements across the country in 2004 would show the following panoply of different service structures, each with their own different systems of pay, terms, and management. It is still a fragmented and muddled picture. We have the following.

- Independent counselling organizations delivering counselling to the NHS with self-employed counsellors on hourly rates as varied as £15 to £50 per hour.
- Managed counselling services within the NHS with self-employed counsellors, again paid at varied hourly rates with wildly different supervision arrangements. Sometimes supervision is paid for, sometimes not. Sometimes administrative time is covered, sometimes not.

- Managed counselling services within Mental Health Trusts or Primary Care Trusts with counsellors employed, but often paid well below their psychology and CPN counterparts. (The range for a full-time basic practice counsellor is between £21,000 and £28,000 per annum.)
- No counselling provision at all, but various 'catch all' primary care mental health professionals who are not trained to undertake psychological therapy.

The various 'pay scales' that are currently used for employed counsellors are imaginative, to say the least, ranging from locally agreed counsellor scales to CPN or psychology scales to administration and clerical rates! We have even heard anecdotally of a counsellor being employed on the same rates as the maintenance staff. That this still remains the case in the modern NHS is shocking. As we write, with Agenda for Change bandings for counsellor posts established, there is hope for the first time that counsellors will be integrated alongside other health professionals in a single equitable pay and banding system. However, the situation for counsellors in 2005 is still uncertain, insecure, and inconsistent as the following illustrations will show.

A tale of two counsellors

Marjorie

Marjorie is 52 and qualified as a counsellor in 1984 having done her initial training with Relate. Before this she had worked as a special needs teacher. She subsequently undertook a further degree training in psychodynamic counselling at her local university. She worked initially as a Relate counsellor, and also for a voluntary organization providing counselling for young people. For the past fourteen years she has been working in private practice and latterly for nine years in primary care. Initially, her contract was as a self-employed counsellor attached to a practice comprising 15,000 patients. She was contracted by the fund-holding practice and employed for ten hours a week at a rate of £15.00 per hour in 1996. There was no financial provision for supervision, although she was allowed supervision within her working time. All hours were deemed clinical and she carried out her own administration outside these paid hours. She had no management and no formal links with other counsellors in her area. She gets on well with her GP colleagues but rarely sees them or other colleagues in the practice.

Her hourly rate had risen to £21 per hour by 2002, when the PCT decided they needed to restructure the counselling provision. This is still work in progress, and the aim of the PCT is to move all counsellors into a managed service of employment by the end of 2005 to work alongside graduate mental health workers and gateway workers. It is proving to be a painful and muddled process. Marjorie has got a wealth of experience and clinical knowledge and is a very senior practitioner. She wants to ensure that she is properly remunerated for her experience if she moves to an employed contract and that she can retain clinical autonomy. She is currently seeking help and support from her professional body, Counsellors in Primary Care, and from BACP, of which she is also an accredited member. She is worried that a move to employment will bring a loss of pay and no real benefit to herself.

Jackie

Jackie is 38 and qualified as a counsellor fairly recently (1999). She previously worked in the private sector in employment recruitment. She has an advanced diploma and subsequent MA from a private psychotherapy and counselling training institute. Her modality is integrative. In 2001, Karen applied for a part-time post in primary care, which was advertised nationally, having done a managed clinical placement in general practice as part of her MA year's training shortly after qualifying with her diploma. She got the post and was appointed on a local grading scale as a practice counsellor Band 5 rising to Band 6 in 2004. She is currently employed in a 0.5 post at full-time equivalent salary of £28,000 p.a (2005).

Jackie's supervision is provided in-house and she receives weekly group supervision (in a group of three for 1.5 hours a week) from a supervisor who is also employed within the service at Band 7 (part time, 0.4). Her contract stipulates that she should work a ratio of 70% clinical hours to 30% administrative hours, and she is managed by the counselling service manager (full time, Band 8d). She is employed directly by the PCT within which the counselling service is managed with the primary care directorate. There are twelve other counsellors and three supervisors employed within the service in this PCT. The counselling service manager also manages the new graduate workers and has introduced mental health team working in most of the practices, to include the counsellor, GPs, CPN, and Graduate Mental Health Worker. Jackie is able to access regular in-house CPD training and attend agreed conferences and external CPD in line with her personal appraisal. She meets her counselling colleagues on a monthly basis and has regular multi-disciplinary meetings within the practice and the Mental Health Trust. Jackie is a registered member of CPC. She is interested in undertaking management training in the future as she would like to work towards heading a service either in the NHS or in the private sector.

Marjorie says:

> I am glad that the PCT is restructuring the service as I felt very professionally isolated before. However, I have always had good relations with my GPs and other colleagues in the team and I am worried that I will lose this. We seem to be becoming more separate. Also, I had good clinical freedom – basically I could offer patients the sort of length of therapy they needed, within reasonable limits, based on my assessment. My GPs were happy with this and were able to provide it under fund-holding. Now I am worried that I will only be able to offer time-limited work and what will happen to those patients that need more time? I am looking forward to having my supervision and training paid for and to having greater security for the service as a whole. I think it is excellent that more counsellors are coming into the service and that all the practices will have access to counselling. I am not convinced that being employed is going to be of great benefit to me but I can accept that it helps overall. But the PCT must appoint a clinical manager, otherwise I am not at all sure that the things that are important for a counselling service will be properly represented.

Jackie says:

> I feel reasonably secure and supported in this post and it is good to have other counselling colleagues in the service

overall. I think I was fortunate to get one of these appointments, particularly in a service that was just developing. The counselling service manager is a psychodynamic counsellor and she really seems to understand how to pick her way through the myriad difficulties of being a manger in the NHS. There are still lots of problems – we don't have enough clinical hours overall for a start – but I don't feel personally under too much pressure to make everything all right! I can only do what I am contracted to do as best I can. Using CORE helps us a lot, I think, as it shows where the work we do is effective and helps make a case for full service levels. I find it useful for reflecting on my own individual work too. I like working across the team with other mental health practitioners too . . . I think they have a lot more respect for counsellors now we are working more closely together. I am worried about the new NICE guidelines – they seem so formulaic and I would be really worried if counselling had to be seen to be another schematic treatment option in order to survive. In fact, it is just the opposite in practice. When we all work together we all become more reflective, which can only be a good thing surely?

Marjorie and Jackie's circumstances are indeed very different. However they both do the same work right now, right here in the NHS in the UK. They both work in general practice, see the same range of patients, collaborate with GPs and other health professionals, undertake assessments, use referral pathways, keep records and notes, attend regular supervision, CPD, etc., manage their counselling work in a highly complex setting, and depend on the help and support of others as well as their own high level of training in order to do this work. They also both want the same things – a place in the scheme of things to offer patients the possibility of good psychological thera-peutic treatment within a setting that allows for reflective practice and a chance to work closely with their colleagues . . . not too much to ask surely?

Time for change

In 2003 the DoH, under the Agenda for Change banner, set out its proposals for a new approach to the NHS pay and grading systems to replace the various existing systems. The intentions of Agenda for Change (DoH, 2003) are that it will

- Lead to more patients being treated more quickly and being given higher quality care;
- Assist new ways of working that best deliver the range and quality of services required, in as efficient and effective a way as possible and organized to meet the needs of patients;
- Assist the goal of achieving a quality workforce with the right numbers of staff, with the right skills and diversity and organized in the right way;
- Improve all aspects of equal opportunity and diver-sity, especially in the areas of career and training opportunities and working patterns that are flexible to accommodate family commitments;
- Meet equal pay for work of equal value criteria, recog-nizing that pay constitutes any benefits in cash or conditions;
- Implement the new pay system within the manage-ment, financial, and service constraints likely to be in place.

So that's all fine then . . . except that neither counsellors nor adult psychotherapists have existed within any pay and grading frameworks within the NHS until now. Agenda for Change holds the key for counselling posts to be finally put on the grading map in terms *of equal pay for work of equal value criteria*. As we write, the job profiles for counsellors in the NHS have been agreed. From implementation, all counsellors should be able to align themselves through matching to the right band for their job. For the first time counsellors EXIST in the NHS!

The philosophical

Another way of looking at the impact of psychological therapy in primary care raised at the beginning of this chapter is to think about the very different paradigms of medical and psychological therapeutic practice. What difference has psychological thinking brought to medical practice and vice versa? Do we learn and benefit from working with each other or do we obstruct and impede each other – or is the truth somewhere in the middle? It is interesting to reflect on something that permeates the whole question of managing and resourcing counselling in primary care:

> Have counsellors compromised themselves in their efforts to fit into the NHS and second, if there is evidence of such compromise, is it an inevitable consequence of two very different models (the medical and the psychotherapeutic) meeting in one setting? [Foster, 2004]

Our friendly, open minded GP, Simon, might say in answer:

Sometimes I get impatient with the counsellor because I think she is unrealistic. General practice is a really busy place and we haven't always got time to talk about every single patient at length. It seems amazing to me that counsellors can have fifty minutes with each patient and with no interruptions! I'm lucky if I get five minutes . . . but on the other hand I really value the help I get from the counsellor with certain patients – it's a real relief for me to know that a troubled patient can be seen in the surgery and that I can talk to the counsellor easily about their progress. We have introduced regular mental health practice team meetings and these are really useful – the counsellor, GPs, CPNs and graduate workers all attend these. We never challenge whether therapy should be done at all – there is plenty of evidence to support it – but rather try to look at matching the right level or type of treatment to the patient. This includes medication right through to long-term psychotherapy.

Experience shows us that the successful integration of counselling practice into primary care depends on the following:

- a counsellor who is available to colleagues and can make good working relationships;
- a degree of education in the practice as to what sort of people can make good use of counselling;
- working as a team not as separate individuals;
- sharing information and supporting each other;
- maintaining clear boundaries and distinguishing between collaboration and confidentiality;
- believing that everyone is doing their best and that when they are not they need help, not blame;

- regularly reviewing practice together using audit and outcome evaluation.

Dave Packwood a counselling service manager in Sandwell, near Birmingham, describes just such a system where GPs, CPNs and counsellors are all on-side and making fascinating changes to their primary mental health services in terms of integration that are aimed at the service users in their patch.

> A good deal of my thinking has gone into the development of this new model for the primary care mental health services . . . The new team will be re-branded as the 'Well Being and Mental Health Service', to reflect a more holistic approach and to soften the stigmatising mental health component. Basically everyone, where possible, will be chucked out into the new health centres to form the team. This will include as much as possible of the traditional secondary services. It is envisaged that this component may roll on over several years to include more and more of existing services.
>
> The approach will be holistic, being reactive to individual needs and contexts. It will seek to offer genuine choice. . . . A patient will be able to explore and choose from a range of options in conjunction with their assessor/s. We are currently researching the availability of local alternative therapies. The PCT has allocated money so that existing staff can train in alternative approaches, where these are indicated by the evidence base.
> It is intended that the work will be genuinely team based, with lashings of co-working and trans-professional consultation. [Packwood, 2004]

This is radical stuff indeed, but is simply an extension of establishing counselling in primary care and then integrating mental health practitioners from both primary and secondary care, and that includes GPs of course. We love the way Dave cheerfully speaks of 'chucking everyone out into the new centres to form the team'! My guess is that such positive developments can only be tenable for services such as this where the thinking and the planning is done once good relations have been established between all parties and all parties are included in the process. It is also necessary to have the personnel in place. Having said this, it is more than possible to get a well-regulated and integrated approach to primary care mental health that allows for separate professional boundaries to be maintained and a degree of trust to develop while placing the patient at the centre. This is like a parallel to the process of therapy itself. It is based on making relationships and *takes place over time.*

The political

Which brings us neatly to the political dimension where time is not often given house-room! The recent NICE guidelines on both depression and anxiety indicate a frightening adherence to schematic, one-size-fits-all, quick-fix solution-based approaches to the treatment of these all too human conditions. These are very different to the reality of primary care described by Launer and others, above. When it comes to mental health, and indeed physical health treatment, the reality is much more complex. Counsellors in primary care, together with their GP colleagues, generally reflect this and encourage a cohesive approach to symptoms. The patient is held to be central, not the problem or the symptom(s):

The characteristics that distinguish effective and efficient primary care are its accessible front line position, its longitudinal nature, its focus on the individual, its responsibility for dealing with most common problems in the population, its co-ordinating function for integrated patient care and its orientation to prevention in addition to traditional clinical functions. [Royal College of General Practitioners, 1996]

Compare this with a position that insists on symptom relief (through medication or schematic therapy) in a fixed period of time. This is a very different way of analysing treatment and effectiveness. Much has been written already of the tendency to prescribe psychotropic drugs to change the way patients feel about a situation rather than helping them deal with their problems. Much has also been revealed of late to indicate that the prescribing of selective serotonin reuptake inhibitors (SSRIs) has not been the safe catch-all it might have appeared. The costs to the NHS of over prescribing, of mis-prescribing and non-compliance are colossal. The counselling route may seem to be the harder, longer, messier route, but it is one that must be firmly held in mind as an option in today's NHS. It is safe, effective, and modest in cost and, more importantly, in intent. None of the randomized control trials (a blunt instrument for the purposes of researching psychological processes) under-taken to compare counselling with ordinary GP care found that the cost of counselling was markedly different than those associated with patients under 'usual GP care' (Friedl, King, & Lloyd, 2000; Harvey *et al.*, 1998; Ward *et al.*, 2000) but *the experience* is very different for the patient. Interestingly, compliance rates with general practice coun-selling are far lower than GP attendance, which we might expect, but altogether lower than that of compliance with relevant prescribed medication. Also the presence of a counsellor in a practice has a notable affect on prescribing patterns and the number of patient presentations to GPs (Hudson-Allez, 1997).

There are always constraints in the NHS – most notably that of money and consequently of staff – that put a time and money pressure on every resource. Counselling, however, is very cost effective over the long term and when compared to other calls on primary care. Nevertheless, it is all too easily squeezed out because of pressures to produce instant results and to reduce waiting times. Arguments are made about the costs of resourcing a primary care mental health team with professional counsellors and other key workers, but these are not high when compared with rocketing prescription costs. At the same time we are seeing a rise in referrals affected by the raising of people's expectations of things that are not always possible. While primary care counselling tries to hold firm to its bedrock of clinically based good practice, newly designed graduate workers are being introduced with little training and no evidence base. While these newly designed workers may well prove useful in primary care they are an additional and limited resource.

The Sainsbury Centre warned in its review in 2003 that

> The intentions of the NHS plan [to introduce 1000 new mental health workers into primary care in 2004] are welcomed. However experience suggests that the remit of these new posts will become confused unless the aims are clarified at the beginning . . . the role of the new mental health workers is clearly limited to providing explicit,

evidence based forms of psychological interventions to individuals who have specific mental health problems. They should not be involved in assessment ... integration into the primary care counselling service is essential. Management, supervision and mentoring could also be provided by the counselling service. [Sainsbury Centre, 2003]

Meanwhile, mental health policy from Nimhe tends to be designed largely from the secondary service model of care pathways and diagnosis. Despite the inroads individual GPs and counsellors are making on mental health awareness in primary care and on effective treatment and outcome this seems to be having very little impact on the formation of mental health policy at the top. Paradoxically however it could be very helpful to our 'leaders' since one of the most useful and necessary functions of psychological therapy is that the ball is firmly put back in the individual's court and work is done on an acceptance of limits

In their report *Cases for Change* (Nimhe, 2003) refers to barriers to change and asks 'What is preventing change (in relation to mental health services) from taking place – if we know what the problems are why haven't we been able to develop successful solutions?' They go on to ask:

- is there the political will?
- is there financial support to implement change?
- are issues concerned a priority for workers?
- do the challenges feel surmountable?

We would add other questions to this. Has Nimhe not noticed that radical change is already taking place in relation to the treatment and approach to mental health in primary care in the guise of the development of primary care counselling and psychotherapy with considerable support from GPs? Why is there still a lack of will and ignorance in relation to resourcing these proven and effective approaches to mental health that are already in place in many parts of the country? To paraphrase Balint, the eminent GP of the 1960s, the more one knows of the problems of general practice, the more impressed one becomes by the immediate need for psychotherapy. Forty years later we still don't seem to be impressed enough!

We can only conclude at this point that the political movers and shakers might well be looking in the wrong place for many of their answers and missing the point that a lot of what works effectively in primary care mental health is already in place under the guise of established and fledgling primary care counselling services. This is a rich vein, as yet in many places not fully tapped. Not only do counselling services offer invaluable talking therapy treatments but also sources of training and supervision for other non-specialist primary care health professionals. But before you can dig deep you must ensure your mine is safe and secure!

On that expectant note, whether you are a counselling manager, a trust manager, a GP, or counsellor, we hope this book will help you design, resource, and continue to manage your counselling services as best you can with the best interests of ordinary people – counselling colleagues, medical colleagues, and patients, in mind.

Summary

Whatever is going to work best in the NHS with regard to changes in mental health services is going to come about by giving time and thought to the making of collaborative, cross-professional relationships between colleagues, between clinicians and patients, and between managers and clinicians. Counselling and psychological therapy works relationally. Counsellors in general practice can make the biggest impact on patient care when they keep this in mind. To sum up, by way of parody . . . it's the relationship stupid . . .

REFERENCES

Association of Counsellors and Psychotherapists in Primary Care (2004). *CPC: Guidelines and Protocols*. Bognor Regis: CPC.

Burton, J., & Launer, J. (Eds.) (2003). *Supervision and Support in Primary Care*. Oxford: Radcliffe Medical Press.

Butterton, M., & Murphy, A. (2002). *The Search for a New Model of Clinical Supervision in a Primary Care Setting. CPC Monograph 1: Supervision*. Bognor Regis: CPC.

Caroll, M. (1996). *Counselling Supervision: Theory, Skills and Practice*. London: Cassell.

CPC (2004). *Association of Counsellors and Psychotherapists in Primary Care Code of Ethical Principles* (revised).

DoH (1997). *The New NHS: Modern, Dependable*. London: HMSO.

DoH (1999). *National Service Framework (NSF) for Mental Health*. London. DoH.

DoH (2000). *The New NHS*.

DoH (2001). *Treatment Choice in Psychological Therapies and Counselling: Evidence Based Clinical Practice Guideline*. London: DoH.

DoH (2003). *Improving Quality in Primary Care: A Practical Guide to the National Service Framework for Mental Health*

DoH (2003). *Agenda for Change: Proposed Agreement*. London: DoH.

DoH (2004). *Organising and Delivering Psychological Therapies*.

Donaldson (1998).

Foster, J. (2004). *Psychodynamic Practice*, *10*(3): 301.

Foster, J., & Murphy, A. (2004). *CPC Guidance and Frameworks for a Managed Primary Care Counselling Service*. Bognor Regis: CPC.

Friedl, K., King, M., & Lloyd, M. (2000). The economics of employing a counsellor in general practice; analysis of data from a randomised control trial. *British Journal of General Practice, 50*: 276–283.

Harvey, I., Nelson, S., Lyons, R., Unwin, C., Monaghan S., & Peters, T. (1998). A randomised controlled trial and economic evaluation of counselling in primary care. *British Journal of General Practice, 48*: 1043–1048.

Hawkins, P., & Shohut, R. (1989). *Supervision in the Helping Professions*. Buckingham: Open University Press.

Hess, A. K. (1980). *Psychotherapy Supervision: Theory, Research and Practice*. New York: Wiley.

Hudson-Allez, G. (1997). *Time Limited Therapy in a General Practice Setting*. London: Sage.

Loganbill, C., Hardy, G. E., & Delworth, U. (1982). Supervision: A Conceptual Model. *The Counselling Psychologist, 10*: 3–42.

Main, T. (1957). The ailment. In: T. Main (Ed.), *The Ailment and Other Psychoanalytic Essays*. London: Free Association Books.

Marsh, G. N., & Barr, J. (1975). Marriage Guidance counselling in a group practice. *Journal of the Royal College of General Practitioners, 25*: 73–75.

Mellor-Clark, J. et al, (2001). Counselling outcomes in primary health care: A CORE system data profile. *European Journal of Psychotherapy, Counselling and Health, 4*: 65–86.

Mellor-Clark, J., Simms-Ellis R., & Burton, M. (2001). National survey of counsellors working in primary care: evidence for growing professionalisation? Royal College of General Practitioners.

Mendlewicz, J. (2001). *British Journal of Psychiatry*. 179.

National Institute for Mental Health in England (2003). *Cases for Change. A Review of the Foundations of Mental Health Policy and Practice 1997–2002*. DoH (2001)

Packwood, D. (2004) *CPC Review, 5*(3).

Proctor, B. (undated). Supervision: A co-operative exercise in accountability. In: M. Marken & M. Payne (Eds.), *Enabling and Ensuring*. Leicester: National Youth Bureau and Council for Education and Training in Youth and Community Work.

Royal College of General Practitioners (1996). *The Nature of General Practice*.

Sainsbury Centre for Mental Health (2003). *Primary Solutions: An Independent Policy Review on the Development of Primary Care Mental Health Services*. London: SCMH.

Sibbald, B., Addington-Hall, J., Brenneman, D., & Freeling, P. (1993). Counsellors in English and Welsh practices, their nature and distribution. *British Medical Journal, 306*: 29–33.

Snape, C., Perren, S., Jones, L., & Rowland, N. (2003). Counselling – why not? A qualitative study of people's accounts of not taking up counselling appointments. *Counselling and Psychotherapy Research, 3*(3): 239–245.

Ward, E., King, M., et al. (2000). Randomised controlled trial of non-directive counselling, cognitive behaviour therapy and usual GP care for patients with depression. ii Cost effectiveness. *British Medical Journal, 321*.

Wells, B. (2004). The Counselling Service Manager's View. *CPC Review, 5*(1).

APPENDICES

APPENDIX 1

Job Description CPC Grade 1 Counsellor
Agenda for Change Band 5 Counsellor

Job statement

1. Provides counselling directly to patients/clients.
2. Manages a caseload and maintains patient/client records.
3. Working towards registration with relevant professional body.

Job description

1. Provides counselling to the designated NHS service users in the designated setting. For example – adults/children/the elderly/primary care/a specialist service.
2. Assesses the appropriateness of counselling for service users – conducts initial assessment for confirmation of presenting problem and suitability for treatment and monitoring over agreed period of counselling.
3. To fulfil professional clinical supervision requirements.
4. To attend service meetings as required.
5. Plan and organise own caseload.
6. To maintain adequate records of clinical work and provide appropriate statistical returns as required.
7. Sets and delivers therapy to meet the needs of individual patients/clients.

8. Follows national and organisational policies applicable to role including those implemented as a result of legislative changes, may comment on changes in administrative procedures.
9. Works with clients independently within policies and codes of conduct.
10. To assist in the evaluation of the service by contributing to data collection and analysis and to participate in research as required.
11. To maintain training and continue professional development.
12. To liaise with other NHS professionals and colleagues working in psychological therapies
13. To participate in any other activities as agreed with the service managers.
14. To be aware of and comply with the policies, procedures and service standards of the employing NHS Trust.

Person Specification: Grade 1/ Band 5 Counsellor

Essential criteria

■ Recognised professional qualification in counselling/ psychotherapy or counselling psychology diploma level or equivalent. For example, BACP recognised course or equivalent (i.e. minimum 450 hours skills and theory, 120 hours of supervised practice, 40 hours of personal therapy).
■ Ability to make use of clinical supervision (evidenced by a counselling supervisor's statement).

- Ability to maintain confidentiality appropriate to the setting.
- Competency in working within a recognised theoretical framework.
- Ability to work within a time limit.
- Effective communication skills both orally and in writing.
- Ability to work effectively with colleagues from other disciplines.

Desirable criteria

- Previous experience working in primary care or other healthcare settings and/or significant life experience.
- Eligibility for BACP accreditation (or equivalent registration) or evidence of working towards this status.
- Experience of contributing to service evaluation.
- Experience of using audit and evaluation systems.

Job Description CPC Grade 2
Counsellor
Agenda for Change Band 6 Counsellor

Job statement:

1. Assesses and provides counselling to patients/clients
2. Manages a case load and maintains patient/ client records
3. Provides mentoring (professional support and guidance) to pre-registration counsellors, trainees, students
4. May work in a particular field

Job description:

1. Provides counselling to the designated NHS service users. For example: adults/children/the elderly/a specialist service
2. Undertakes initial assessment of clients presenting with multiple and complex issues; selection of appropriate therapeutic treatment, decisions regarding referrals to specialist services
3. Fulfils professional clinical supervision requirements
4. Manages own caseload
5. Maintains professional accreditation and/or registration
6. Delivers programmes of care. Sets and delivers therapeutic treatment to meet the needs of individual clients
7. Attends service meetings as required.
8. Maintains adequate records of clinical work and provide appropriate statistical returns as required.

9. Assists in the evaluation of the service by contributing to data collection and analysis and to participate in research as required.

10. Follows national and organisational policies, may comment on changes in administrative procedures/ implements policies relating to provision of counselling services, proposes changes to service delivery and working practices.

11. Works with clients independently within policies and codes of conduct/ interprets policies in relation to community caseload.

12. Maintains training and continued professional development.

13. Develops expertise in a specific area of counselling - for example, counselling supervision, group work, or other specialism.

14. May offer support, monitoring and induction of pre-registration counsellors, trainees, students undertaking placements; provides training in counselling/ mentoring to Grade 1 counsellors and/or counsellors on placements.

15. May take specific responsibility for some area of practise within the service.

16. Liaises with other NHS professionals and colleagues working in psychological therapies.

17. Participates in any other activities as agreed with the service managers.

18. Is aware of and complies with the policies, procedures and service standards of the employing Trust.

Person Specification – Grade 2/ Band 6 Counsellor

Essential criteria

■ Recognised professional qualification to diploma level or equivalent. For example, BACP recognised course or equivalent (i.e. minimum 450 hours skills and theory, 120 hours of supervised practice, 40 hours of personal therapy).

■ Knowledge of the full range of counselling procedures and techniques acquired through professional diploma, advanced diploma/accreditation/registration or further substantial training and accredited clinical supervision plus experience.

■ Knowledge and familiarity with the organisational setting of the NHS and with current policy with respect to Mental Health services.

■ Is currently an Accredited Practitioner recognised by a national professional body.

■ Is able to offer specific professional expertise dependant on experience.

■ Is able to offer mentoring to counsellors on placement

■ Ability to make use of clinical supervision (evidenced by a counselling supervisor's statement).

■ Ability to maintain confidentiality appropriate to the setting.

■ Competency in working within a recognised theoretical framework.

■ Ability to work within a time limit.

■ Effective communication skills both orally and in writing.

■ Ability to work effectively with colleagues from other disciplines.

Desirable criteria:

- Experience of contributing to service evaluation.
- Experience of using audit and evaluation methods.
- Experience of undertaking professional research.

Job Description: Senior Counsellor
CPC Grade 3
Agenda for Change Counsellor Specialist
Band 7

Job statement:

1. Provides specialist counselling to patients/ clients e.g. post traumatic stress, conflict resolution.
2. Manages a specialist case load and maintains patient/ client records.
3. Provides professional/ clinical supervision to, acts as professional lead for, pre-registration counsellors, trainees, students; may coordinate team of counsellors; may co-ordinate training; may undertake research.

Job description:

1. To provide counselling to designated NHS service users for example – adults/children/the elderly/a specialist service.
2. To take responsibility for a specialist sector of the counselling service – for example education, counselling supervision, research, specialist expertise and training.
3. To organise own and team workload, organise induction, training and CPD programmes
4. To work with clients independently, within policies and codes of conduct. May be lead specialist.
5. To share some management roles including deputising for service manager or locality lead.

6. Implement policies relating to provision of counselling services, proposes changes to service delivery/ contributes to policy discussions at wider organisational level.

7. To assess the appropriateness of counselling for service users and to work with service users presenting with more complex problems e.g. providing therapy to difficult individuals. To undertake initial assessment of clients presenting with multiple and complex issues; selection of appropriate therapeutic treatment, decisions regarding referrals to specialist services.

8. Develop and deliver therapeutic treatment of complex cases with multiple presenting problems/co morbidity. Deliver specialist therapeutic treatment to meet the needs of individual clients e.g. treatment of phobias, critical incident de-briefing, post trauma counselling, therapeutic group work; counselling the terminally ill.

9. Provide specialist advice and training to other disciplines/services.

10. Fulfil professional clinical supervision requirements.

11. Maintain professional accreditation and/or registration

12. Organise and attend team/service meetings as required.

13. Maintain adequate records of clinical work and provide appropriate statistical returns as required.

14. Assist in the evaluation of the service by contributing to data collection and analysis and to participate in research as required. Complete regular waiting list audits and case load statistics. Undertake complex audits, participate in research activities/carry out research projects in own specialist area.

15. Maintain training and continue professional development.
16. Have expertise in a specific area of counselling and to contribute significantly to service development
17. Offer mentoring to other Grades of counsellors and/or counsellors on placements. Provide clinical supervision to a range of counsellors; support and monitor pre-registration counsellors, trainees, students undertaking placements/ provide specialist training to other disciplines
18. Liaise with other NHS professionals and colleagues working in psychological therapies
19. Participate in any other activities as agreed with the service managers.
20. Be aware of and comply with the policies, procedures and service standards of the employing Trust.

Person Specification – Grade 3/Band 7 Senior Counsellor

Essential criteria

- Recognised professional qualification to diploma level or equivalent. For example, BACP recognised course or equivalent (i.e. 450 hours skills and theory, 120 hours of supervised practice, 20 hours of personal therapy)
- Knowledge of the full range of counselling procedures and techniques plus knowledge of specialist therapeutic techniques acquired through professional diploma, advanced diploma/accreditation/registration or further substantial training and accredited clinical

supervision plus experience plus further specialist courses to master's or equivalent level

- Currently be an Accredited Practitioner recognised by a national professional body
- To offer specific professional expertise dependent on experience
- To be able to offer mentoring to counsellors on placement
- Ability to make use of clinical supervision (evidenced by a counselling supervisor's statement)
- Ability to maintain confidentiality appropriate to the setting
- Competency in working within a variety of recognised theoretical frameworks and knowledge of other ways of working
- Ability to work within a time limit
- Effective communication skills both orally and in writing
- Management and implementation skills/experience
- Overview of current professional issues
- Comprehensive knowledge of the NHS organisation and DoH policy regarding mental health services
- Ability to work effectively with colleagues from other disciplines
- Experience of audit and research and the presentation of findings
- Experience of audit and outcome evaluation approaches

CPC Grade 4 – Project Manager, Section Leader – Band 8, Range a–b (12 points)

Agenda for Change – profile not yet signed off.

Provisional job statement:

Will carry out management responsibilities under a department head/service manager

1. Advise on appointment of counsellors, policy and protocols.
2. Manage and monitor the professional development of Counsellors.
3. Lead on new projects and service development
4. Continue to maintain some clinical practice.
5. Audit and evaluate the counselling service.

CPC Grade 5 – Service Manager – Band 8 range c–d (12 points)

Agenda for Change – profile not yet signed off.

Provisional job statement:

Will manage the counselling service:

1. Be responsible for appointment of counsellors, supervisors, project managers
2. Be responsible for strategy and service development
3. Operate at senior management level within the PCT/ Mental Health Trust
4. Be responsible for staff development

5. Be responsible for audit and evaluation and service budget
6. Write annual reports for the Trust or Governing Body.
7. Maintain role in relation to national developments

APPENDIX 2a: Choosing and using the CORE system

At an early stage in the service development, Linda had impressed upon Alison the importance of audit and evaluation data, and together they'd explored their attitudes towards it. For Linda, as the Commissioning Manager, she'd explained that it was increasingly difficult to purchase services that couldn't provide robust evidence of the effectiveness of their outcomes and their continuing commitment to developing service quality. Linda explained at length how the whole of the NHS was increasingly standards-led, and how clinical governance was making everyone (irrespective of their role or rank) accountable for the part they played in the overall quality of local healthcare delivery – including the GPs. In response, Alison explained how her training had taught her the central importance of 'trust' in developing relationships with clients, referrers, supervisors, and managers. Against such a background, Linda was able to appreciate how the 'new NHS' concepts of *measurement, monitoring, quality performance management* were at odds with the culture of counselling, and how important it would be to embrace the strengths of such a cultural heritage rather than fight against it in introducing change.

In response, together they spent time reflecting on the implications of some of the key messages in publications such as the *National Service Framework for Mental Health* (DoH, 1999); *Treatment Choice in Psychological Therapies and Counselling* (DoH, 2001); and *Organising and Delivering Psychological Therapies* (DoH, 2004). As Alison began to understand some of the pressures Linda was under to provide 'evidence' to support her decision to create the new counselling service, she also began to realize that such evidence wasn't just a one-off need, or something that was targeted specifically at counselling. Alison quickly realized it was something that all health service providers would need to build into their ongoing professional relationships with their commissioners. From these early explorations and discussions it became obvious that 'good' audit and evaluation wasn't about being seen to be doing the right thing, but as a major investment in the service's future, it was more about doing the right thing right! Consequently, both Linda and Alison thought very carefully about what approach would offer the greatest benefit for the considerable effort that all would need to invest.

Weighing up the various audit and evaluation method options available to them, Linda and Alison spent time on a three-stage assessment exercise. In the first stage they identified the range of approaches they could adopt. In the second stage they identified five key criteria by which to assess the relative cost-benefit of each option, and in the third and final stage they assessed each option against the key criteria.

Linda and Alison's identified audit and evaluation options

- Use a traditional in-house client satisfaction/exit questionnaire.

- Use a recognized pre- and post-counselling/psychological therapy client self-report outcome measure such as The General Heath Questionnaire, The Beck Depression Inventory or the Hospital Anxiety and Depression Scale.
- Use the nationally standardized system – CORE.
- Develop and use a local system.

Linda and Alison's audit and evaluation method assessment criteria

- Evaluation tools must be affordable and easy to use for both practitioners and clients.
- Must provide evidence to demonstrate the *effectiveness* of counselling as recommended by the *National Service Framework Standard 2*.
- Must provide evidence to demonstrate the *safety* of the service by demonstrating high quality risk assessment as recommended by the *National Service Framework Standard 7*.
- Must provide information to develop the *service quality* domains recommended by the DoH guidelines *Organising and Delivering Psychological Therapies* (e.g. referral equity, waiting times, and low DNA's and unplanned endings).
- Resultant data must be easy to analyse, interpret and report to meet clinical governance requirements.

Table 1. Linda and Alison's audit and evaluation method assessment

Assessment criteria	Evaluation method options			
	Satisfaction/exit questionnaires	Pre/post counselling self-report outcome measures	The CORE system	Developing an in-house local system
Ease of **access and use**	*Strength*: Easy to design and use and a familiar and acceptable approach to counsellors. *Weakness*: Info only from clients willing to return questionnaires (often reported to be less than 50%)	*Strength*: Traditional research method with proven track record of clinical utility. *Weakness*: Time-consuming, and high-quality free questionnaires are limited in number	*Strength*: Nationally recognized standard in widescale use and free for photocopying. *Weakness*: Deceptively sophisticated, reported to require training for best use and utility	*Strength*: Can be designed to include data to help maximise practitioner engagement *Weakness*: Requires some research expertise to design and will be time-consuming to pilot and perfect.
Must provide evidence to demonstrate the **effectiveness** of counselling	*Strength*: Should demonstrate the extent to which counselling has helped meet clients' needs *Weakness*: Found by research to suffer from a 'halo effect' where clients are reluctant to criticise	*Strength*: Should demonstrate counselling benefits in symptom reduction and/or enhanced quality of life. *Weakness*: 'Outcomes' known only for clients with two questionnaires	*Strength*: Provides 'evidence' on effectiveness from both client and practitioner perspectives *Weakness*: Requires some research expertise to analyse and interpret, or fee-based CORE-PC software	As above

(continued)

Table 1. (*continued*)

Assessment criteria	Evaluation method options				
	Satisfaction/exit questionnaires	Pre/post-counselling self–report outcome measures	The CORE system	Developing an in-house local system	
Must provide evidence to demonstrate the **safety** of the service in risk assessment	*Strength:* Can be designed to reflect on safety/risk issues in clients' own terms *Weakness:* Only has a capacity to assess safety retrospectively for those returning questionnaires	**Not applicable** as common outcome measures are not known to contain any risk assessment	*Strength:* Recognized and widely-used objective method of risk assessment *Weakness:* None identified or known	**As above**	
Must provide information to develop **service quality**	*Strength:* Can be designed to reflect on service quality problems/issues in clients' own terms *Weakness:* Info only from clients willing to return questionnaires (often reported to be less than 50%)	**Not applicable** as outcome measures focus only on issues of symptoms and/or quality of life and don't address service quality	*Strength:* Wholly fit for purpose as it's designed as a quality assurance system to develop service quality *Weakness:* Reported to require training to make best use of data for service quality development	**As above**	

(*continued*)

Table 1. (continued)

Assessment criteria	Satisfaction/exit questionnaires	Pre/post-counselling self-report outcome measures	The CORE system	Developing an in-house local system
		Evaluation method options		
Data must be easy to analyse and interpret for clinical governance reports	Strength: Can be designed to include data to focus on info that meets commissioner requirements Weakness: Requires some research expertise to design and will be time-consuming to pilot and perfect.	Not applicable as outcome measures only focus on issues of symptoms and/or quality of life and don't address the domains requisite for clinical governance reports	Strength: Nationally tried and tested clinical governance reporting templates available Weakness: Reported to require training to understand aims and objectives of clinical governance	As above

Linda and Alison's audit and evaluation method assessment

From their assessment (see Table 1), Linda and Alison recognized that while the use of the CORE system carried more resource costs (e.g., staff training and data administration), the overall yield from the time invested in evaluation was significantly greater due to CORE's unique range of support and follow-up services (e.g. CORE-PC analysis and reporting software, National CORE Performance Indicators for benchmarking, and performance management training networks). This careful cost–benefit analysis convinced Linda and Alison that if it was going to be a considerable effort to introduce audit and evaluation into the service, expert support should be highly cost-effective in saving their time, and follow-up support should offer the best possible yield for the (considerable) evaluation effort.

APPENDIX 2b: A profile of the CORE system and support services

THE CORE system tools

CORE OUTCOME MEASURE

This 34-item questionnaire is designed to measure a pan-theoretical 'core' of clients' distress, including subjective well-being, commonly experienced problems or symptoms, and life-social functioning. In addition, items on risk to self and others are included.

By measuring global distress, CORE-OM is suitable for use as an initial screening tool and as an outcome measure. Like most self-report measures it cannot be used to gain a specific diagnosis of a specific disorder. The main purpose of the tool is to offer a global level of distress defined by the average mean score of the 34 items that can be compared with clinical thresholds. The measure has been extensively validated and a series of publications demonstrate that it has considerable utility for both clinical assessment and service evaluation.

CORE THERAPY ASSESSMENT FORM

This double-sided form is designed to capture a 'core' set of contextual information that aids the quality of both client/patient assessment and overall service development.

To enhance patient assessment the form collects important contextual information, including patient/client support; previous/concurrent attendance for psychological therapy; medication; and a categorization system to record presenting difficulties, their impact on day-to-day functioning and any associated risk.

To enhance the development of service quality, the form collects data on critical assessment audit items that profile the accessibility and appropriateness of service provision. These include patient/client demographics, waiting times, and the suitability of referral.

CORE END OF THERAPY FORM

This double-sided form complements the other components of the CORE system to capture a 'core' set of treatment descriptors that aid the interpretation of CORE Outcome Measure scores and (again) inform service development.

To contextualize the outcomes of therapy the form collects profile information that includes therapy length, type of intervention, modality, and frequency.

To enhance the development of service quality, the form collects data on critical discharge audit items that profile the effectiveness and efficiency of service provision. These incude problem and risk review, therapy benefits, session attendance rates, and therapy ending (i.e. planned or unplanned).

CORE system support service

CORE system tools are provided free to UK services on behalf of the CORE System Trust who own the intellectual copyright in the measures and the resultant national data. The Trust license CORE IMS to provide CORE users with high quality support services designed to maximize the local and national yield from the system data.

CORE IMS Ltd provides training and management support to counselling and psychological therapy services using the CORE system. These activities aim to help therapy providers respond to the increasing challenge to improve service quality and demonstrate a commitment to providing effective, efficient, consumer-oriented services. An organization profile is summarized at www.coreims.co.uk

- **Clinical governance/CORE training workshops** introduce managers to the principles and challenges of effective (patient-focused) governance/care. These workshops help managers and practitioners assess their capacity to incorporate the new imperative for transparent and accountable care within their services and place CORE data in a realistic context.

- **CORE-PC** is used by a growing number of UK therapy services to offer direct access to dynamic analytic tools that reward the effort of audit and clinical effectiveness by placing data directly into the hands of service managers and practitioners as and when needed. Articles from users suggest CORE-PC helps engage services in the audit and governance challenge, and offers an active role in shaping services quality as an alternative to the passive acceptance of third-party evaluator, researcher, and/or service inspection assessments.

- A unique set of *National Performance Indicators and Service Descriptors* have helped introduce benchmarking into UK psychological therapy practice. These resources help service to understand the relative quality of their local provision compared with national profiles in key service performance areas such as referral and waiting time management, safe assessment, patient engagement, and (measured) clinical effectiveness.

■ Guided by research findings in the United States, CORE IMS are piloting the introduction of routine *Therapy Performance Appraisal Reports* that provide service managers and supervisors with material that quantifies the quality of individual therapists' work with patients. The introduction of evidence-based performance appraisal helps implement the tenets of clinical governance for psychological therapy provision.

■ CORE IMS also working in collaboration with nationally recognized professional bodies to develop *Service Management and Performance Mentoring Networks* as an e-learning initiative. These have been developed to help service managers access proven effective guidelines for service excellence rather than have to learn by trial and error.

APPENDIX 3

OUTLINE SERVICE SPECIFICATION – COUNSELLING SERVICES CONTENTS

1. Introduction – Aims
2. Scope of Services to be provided
3. Referral Criteria
4. Service Requirements
5. Quality and Monitoring
6. Referral Process
7. Referral Guidelines
8. Training and Development
9. Supervision
10. Administration
11. Record-Keeping
12. Confidentiality
13. Legal Issues
14. Complaints
15. Accessibility
16. Audit and Evaluation
17. Equal Opportunities

SERVICE SPECIFICATION

Central Anywhere PCT Primary Care Counselling Service

1. Introduction

1.1 AIMS

- To provide an accountable, cost effective, managed counselling service for Central Anywhere Primary Care Trust.
- To provide appropriate, professional time limited counselling in primary care.
- To establish effective liaison with secondary and tertiary mental health services.
- To enhance the current provision of primary care counselling in order that all adult service users within the Primary Care Trust have access to counselling in primary care.
- To promote integration within the Primary Care Team.

1.2 BACKGROUND

- Counselling in the Central Anywhere area has become established over the past years with services provided from both the NHS and Private sector.
- The counselling service is available to people who are registered with a Central Anywhere GP (Add Appendix - GP Practices).

2. Scope of services to be provided

2.1 STRUCTURE

- The structure of the service will be in line with national developments. A PCT Counselling Services

Manager will ensure an equitable service across Central Anywhere PCT, using a team of employed counsellors and supervisors.

- The model will be based on individual practice based primary care counsellors. The counsellors will aim to become part of the primary health care team. They will as a norm receive the referrals from within their practice (see section 6 for further discussion of referrals).

- The counsellors will be expected to work as a PCT wide team and will report to the Counselling Services Manager.

- The Counsellors will attend regular supervision with the service supervisors. This will comprise both individual and group supervision.

- The allocation of counselling hours available will be made on a surgery-by-surgery basis, using a calculation of 2 hours per 1000 patient population per week. This will result in an equitable service across the PCT.

- Counselling is to be provided to adults who, in the opinion of their GP, will benefit from a short-term counselling intervention.

- Patients with presenting problems listed in this document (at 6.3) will be referred by their GP to an appropriate counsellor.

- Patients should demonstrate some insight into their problem and show a willingness to explore and deal with their thoughts and feelings.

3. Referral criteria

- GPs will refer patients for counselling within the guidelines set out in the Aims (1.1) and with conditions listed in 6.3 below.

- Patients with enduring mental health problems will not normally be referred to counselling services.

4. Service requirements

The counsellor will be expected to comply with the following:

(a) Be trained to Counselling Diploma standards (minimum 450 hours theory and skills training) and have a minimum of 500 supervised client hours experience. To be either:

■ Accredited by the British Association for Counselling and Psychotherapy (BACP)

■ Registered by Counsellors and Psychotherapists in Primary Care (CPC)

■ Registered with the United Kingdom Council for Psychotherapy (UKCP)

(b) Be a member of a recognized professional body, BACP, CPC or UKCP and be bound by a relevant Code of Ethics and Practice.

(c) Have experience or been trained in time limited counselling and/or primary care counselling. Experience in cognitive–behavioural models would be an advantage.

(d) Have training in and/or have developed skills in assessment and referral, psychiatric awareness and some knowledge of psychotropic drugs.

(e) Be able to provide evidence of professional indemnity insurance cover.

(f) To be aware of current professional practices and a need for their own continued professional development.

(g) To have a minimum of one and a half-hours individual supervision per month, with a suitably qualified and experienced supervisor. The amount of supervision should reflect the amount of work being undertaken by the counsellor. If the counsellor carries a heavy caseload, then more supervision will be required. (See Section 9 for further discussion re supervision.)

(h) The maximum number of sessions anticipated per patient is six to twelve (based on the counselling model of care). If the counsellor feels that this is insufficient on a case-by-case basis, it can be reviewed with the referring GP and the Counselling Services Manager allowing up to a maximum of ten sessions.

(i) Work in a safe environment and be aware of health and safety and risk assessment issues.

(j) Maintain timely and accurate clinical records and provide returns as required by the Counselling Services Manager.

(k) Issue a closure report to the referring GP at the cessation of treatment or on specific request from the GP.

5. *Quality and monitoring*

(a) Reports at PCT and Practice level will be required on a monthly basis, detailing:
    i.   Number of referrals received
    ii. Number of new patients / assessments seen
    iii. Number of DNAs
    iv. Number of closures
    v.   Ethnic origin

(b) A clear statement of those patients who fail to keep their appointments will be established and all DNAs reported promptly to the referring GP.

(c) The Counselling Service Manager will monitor activity levels and individual GP referral patterns.

(d) The service provision will be established to comply with the PCT Clinical Governance responsibilities and subject to clinical audit.

(e) The counselling service will demonstrate an integral routine use of outcome measures with identifiable goals and level of improvement. Outcome measures should preferably be standardised and published. Use of CORE (Clinical Outcomes in Routine Evaluation) as an evaluation tool is a requirement.

(f) The Counsellor will be required to co-operate and participate in any NHS complaint investigation arising from the provision of the counselling service.

6. Referral process

6.1 All referrals should be made in writing. If the referrer wishes to use a specific   counsellor, this should be indicated on the referral letter.

6.2 All referrals must contain the following information:

- Patient's name, date of birth and telephone number.
- Reason for referral.
- Relevant medical history and current medication.
- GP practice.

6.3 Counsellors will see patients with the following presenting problems:

- Pathological bereavement.
- Coping with injury or illness.
- Depression – reactive; circumstantial.

- Developmental or life crisis.
- Emotional, physical or sexual abuse issues.
- Family relationship issues.
- General anxieties and phobias.
- Lack of direction, alienation, existential problems.
- Loss, e.g. relationship, employment, health, etc.
- Self image and identity issues.
- Stress and trauma – pre and post event.
- Issues of sexuality.

6.4 The following may not be suitable for referral to the counselling service:

- Sexual dysfunction.
- Poor communication ability.
- Self-destructive behaviour which, over time, has shown very little change, i.e. prolonged substance misuse, eating disorders.
- Severe mental disorders.
- Severe challenging behaviours, i.e. aggression, violence, severe learning disabilities.

The General Practitioner retains overall medical responsibility for the patient.

Referrals will be made directly to the practice counsellor with a copy sent to the counselling Manager.

7. Referral guidelines

7.1 Taking account of the presenting problems in Section 6, the key criteria for referral are the patient's ability to change and their ego strength. The very fragile may well find counselling too challenging. Those who have too much invested in remaining the same may again find counselling too challenging.

7.2 The counsellor may well, after assessment, re-refer the patient as inappropriate for counselling; suggest a referral to secondary mental health services or some other agency if appropriate (e.g. CRUSE for the recently bereaved).

7.3 The counsellor will work in close collaboration with members of the Primary Health Care Team.

8. Training And Development

8.1 A managed counselling service will ensure on-going and appropriate training and professional development.

8.2 Counsellors will be working in accordance with CPC's Code of Ethical Practice or the equivalent and as such will be aware of the importance of monitoring their own health and safe working practice.

8.3 A managed service will (within budget limitations) be able to provide cover in the case of extended absence.

8.4 It will be the responsibility of the Counsellor to keep professionally updated.

8.5 Counsellors will be expected to attend relevant Primary Care Trust training.

9. Supervision

9.1 All counsellors are required to have on-going professional counselling supervision.

9.2 Counselling supervision is different from clinical case consultations as it takes into account both the therapeutic alliance between counsellor and client, the clinical material and the psychological processes taking place.

9.3 It can be offered in either groups (with the inherent cost savings) or individually.

9.4 Counselling supervisors require training and/or experience in primary care counselling.

9.5 Clinical Psychologists are not trained to provide counselling supervision, though they may provide excellent case supervision.

9.6 Counsellors are required to have a minimum of 1.5 hours individual supervision a month. Supervision needs are to be judged according to caseload and the experience of the clinician.

9.7 Counsellors should not exceed a case-load of more than 20–22 clients a week. This will be regarded as a full-time post. Supervision for such a post will be weekly for one hour minimum.

10. Administration

10.1 Standardized paperwork to be used by all counsellors:

- Counselling Information Leaflet
- Client Attendance Record
- Number of DNAs
- Client Attendance Summary
- Referral Form
- Counsellor/Client Contract
- Discharge Information
- Ethnic Origin

11. Record keeping

11.1 Counsellors are responsible for keeping adequate records as part of the patient's health record in accordance with the practice of the PCT. The Counselling Service Manager is responsible for ensuring the security of counsellor's case notes, which are not part of the patient's records.

11.2 All patient information must be kept on NHS property or at the Surgery where they are based.

11.3 Counsellors will keep a Client Attendance Summary, which provides a brief, one or two sentence summary of each session - this is available to the client, if requested. It is only made available to others with the client's permission.

11.4 Counsellors will ensure their record keeping meets the requirements of the Data Protection Act.

12. Confidentiality

12.1 Counsellors are bound by the CPC Code of Ethics and Practice, which has a confidentiality code that recognises the working links in a Primary Health Care Team.

12.2 Counsellors are required to keep the content of counselling sessions confidential, but they are able to share the process of the sessions with members of the Primary Health Care Team. This will be made explicit in the contract with the client.

12.3 Confidentiality will be broken if there are child protection issues under the Children's Act or issues under the Prevention of Terrorism or Road Traffic Acts.

Confidentiality may also be broken if the counsellor believes that the client is at risk to themselves or others.

13. Legal issues

13.1 Counsellors will be aware of relevant legislation, in particular:

- The Children Act 1989.
- Prevention of Terrorism (Temporary Provisions) Act 1989.
- Road Traffic Act 1988.
- Data Protection Act.
- Consumer Protection Act.

14. Complaints

14.1 It is hoped that most complaints can be resolved via direct discussion between the patient and their counsellor. Where this process proves impossible, the following will apply:

- In the case of patients wishing to complain about their treatment, they should complain in writing to the Practice Manager based in the practice of their referring GP;
- In the case of counsellors wishing to complain about factors relating to the referral process, or aspects concerning the patient, they should address the complaints to the Counselling Service Manager;
- In all cases, complaints will be dealt with in accordance with the local NHS complaint procedure(s).

14.2 In cases of serious or un-resolved complaint, non-performance and arbitration procedures may also apply.

15. Accessibility

15.1 Appointment times: A varied range of possible appointment times will provide a responsive service. (While it is recognized that not all providers will be able to offer all availability, the PCT will wish to ensure that as wide a range of possibilities exist for the benefit of patients.)

15.2 Premises: It is expected that the provision of Counselling Services will be undertaken in GP practice premises that are suitable for the purpose and which can be easily accessed by patients of varying mobility, including disabled access.

16. Audit and evaluation

16.1 The Counselling Service Management will be responsible for effective   Audit and Evaluation within the PCT audit and evaluation procedures.

16.2 Monthly or quarterly monitoring information will be collated to include:

- Number of referrals.
- Number of assessments.
- Number of counselling contracts.
- Number of DNAs.
- Number of discharges.

17. Equal opportunities

17.1 The service is committed to equal opportunities and shall not unlawfully discriminate within the meaning of the Sex Discrimination Act 1975 or the Race Relations Act 1976 in employment.

APPENDIX 4 – Counselling Information Leaflet

Primary care counselling service

Some information to help you decide whether to work with a counsellor

How might counselling help me? People come to counselling to help them deal with a wide variety of difficulties in their lives. You could be facing a crisis in your life such as a relationship problem, bereavement, worry about relatives, or you may feel isolated or lonely. You could be depressed, and not know why, or have trouble coping with past traumas or loss in your life.

What is it like to work with a counsellor? Counselling gives you the opportunity to talk about whatever is troubling you with someone who is not involved in your personal life. Your counsellor will not tell you what to do, but will encourage you to find your own answers. Through exploring your problems with the counsellor, you may find a new way of looking at them, which enables you to face things with more strength and less anxiety. This may help you to take more control of your life and you may then be in a better position to make decisions from the choices available to you.

Can seeing a counsellor make me worse? Counselling may reveal old hurts and wounds that need to be worked through to find more successful ways of resolving difficulties in every day life. This may be a painful process, and you may feel worse before you feel better. And counsellors do not have a magic wand to make everything better;

those changes that do occur will be the ones that you make, in consultation with your counsellor.

What about confidentiality? Counselling is confidential. The only exception to this is if the counsellor believes that there is the possibility of serious harm to yourself or others. In this case the counsellor may be required to breach confidentiality to protect those at risk. The counsellor may wish to discuss some issue with your GP, which would be done with your knowledge. If the counsellor becomes aware that children are at risk, then the counsellor is obliged to take appropriate action. If possible this would be done with your knowledge and consent. Counsellors are not considered to be expert witnesses in a court of law. If you are involved in litigation and chose to make your counselling notes available, they are likely to become public documents.

Where and when will I see my counsellor? The counselling session will take place at the surgery, and usually lasts for fifty minutes. During the first session, if you and your counsellor decide that counselling may be helpful, you will agree on the number of sessions you will work together. This normally requires you to make a commitment to see the counsellor every week.

Complaints: If you wish to make a complaint, please send it in writing to:

The Counselling Service Manager, Central Anywhere PCT

APPENDIX 5 – Notes and confidentiality

The Department of Health has issued a new code of practice on confidentiality. Although the guidelines cover many aspects of confidentiality that counsellors and psychotherapists might feel part of their standard practice, they are now being made explicit in the document. It is stated that the code is also relevant to anyone working in the health area, including those working in the private and voluntary sectors. However, all those working within the confines of the NHS need to establish the working practices of confidentiality that are required by law, ethics, and policy. In particular, it emphasizes that the public

- understand the reasons for processing personal information;
- give their consent for its disclosure;
- trust the way the NHS handles their information;
- understand their rights to access information held about them.

The document points out that confidentiality is a legal obligation derived from case law, that it is already established within professional codes of conduct, and now must be included within all NHS contracts as a specific requirement linked to disciplinary procedures. Where organizational procedures are not in place to facilitate this requirement, staff have to show that they are working within the spirit of this code and making every effort to comply with it.

It argues that anonymized information is not confidential and may be used with relatively few restraints. But information where the individual patient is identified must have the individual's explicit or express consent given freely orally or in writing, and it must only be for healthcare purposes. While medical purposes of access to this information is permitted, disclosures to other agencies for other purposes may not be, unless it is required by law or the courts.

The code reinforces the Caldicott principles of:

- justifying the purpose of disclosure;
- not using patient identifiable information unless absolutely necessary;
- using only the minimum of patient identifiable information, on a strict need-to-know basis;
- everyone being aware of his or her confidentiality responsibilities;
- everyone understanding and complying with the law.

It states that patient notes should be:

- factual, consistent and accurate;
- written as soon as possible after the consultation;
- clear, legible, and in permanent ink;
- dated, timed and signed, with the name of the author printed by the side of the signature;
- presented so that alterations and additions are also dated, timed and signed without obliterating the original entry;
- in clear language so they can be understood by the patient (e.g., no abbreviations);
- able to provide evidence of actions/interventions;
- include the consent to treatment.

Counsellors should not keep patient records at home, but may need to carry some notes with them when attending supervision or case discussion meetings. There have to be agreed procedures for the safeguarding of the information.

Public interest is still included within the terms of this document, referring to Section 60 of the Health & Social Care Act 2001 (see CPC Law Monograph). This article allows the release of patient identifiable information without consent if the circumstances justify over-ruling the right of the individual to confidentiality in order to serve a broader societal interest. In particular, staff are permitted to disclose personal information to prevent a serious crime, support detection, investigation, and punishment of a serious crime, and to prevent abuse or serious harm to others. Such disclosures must be recorded so that clear evidence of the reasoning used and circumstances of the situation can be subsequently reviewed. In these circumstances, the disclosure should be discussed with the patient and permission sought, although this will not be possible in some instances, especially if it involves the investigation of criminal behaviour, as vital evidence may be destroyed.

What constitutes serious crime? Murder, manslaughter, rape, treason, kidnapping, child abuse, serious harm to individuals or the state, or crimes that involve substantial financial loss. Risk of harm is abuse, neglect, road traffic accidents or the spread of infectious diseases. Psychological harm should be considered in addition to physical harm.

The release of such information must be proportionate and reasonable, and it must equate the difference between public interest with what might be of interest to the public.

Patients must now be informed of the information that will be recorded about them in their notes, that it may be shared with other members of the team or with supervisors, and that the information may be used to support clinical audit (e.g., CORE) or other work used to monitor the quality of the care provided. It therefore recommends the use of patient information leaflets, posters, and other materials to inform patients about how information may be shared.

Patients have the right to object to their information being shared in a form that identifies them, even if it is for a healthcare purpose. If patients are deemed competent to make such a decision, and the consequences of that decision have been explained to the patient, then the objection should be respected. This is no different from the right a patient has to refuse treatment.

APPENDIX 6 – Opt-in Letter and Form

Please return to: .... date
Counsellor at (surgery address)

Patient's name and address

Dear

I am writing to confirm that I have received a letter from .... referring you for counselling. Please find enclosed some information about the counselling service at the surgery.

I also enclose a Counselling Appointment Form, which tells you the times I have available and asks how you may be contacted. Could you please complete the form and return it to me at the surgery. Please note that your name will not be placed on the waiting list until the form is returned. At present the waiting list for an initial appointment is approximately .... weeks.

If this is a long time for you to wait, please remember you can always see your GP for support until a counselling appointment becomes available.

If I do not hear from you within four weeks, I will assume you do not wish to have counselling. If you change your mind after that time, you would need to contact your GP for another referral.

Yours sincerely

Practice Counsellor
Primary Care Counselling Service

Reply Page

Please tick the times you can come for counselling. The more times you can tick, the sooner you are likely to be offered an appointment. Certain times are more in demand, and thus the waiting period may be longer for appointments at these times.

Wednesdays:	Thursdays:
10.30	1.30 ....
11.45	2.30 ....
1.00	4.00 ....
	5.00 ....

Please note: If you are unable to make any of these times on a regular basis, you will need to go back to your GP to discuss your referral.

How would you like to be contacted (please tick):
I wish to be contacted only by letter   ☐
I may be contacted by telephone.   ☐

Home telephone no:...
Work/mobile telephone no: ....

If you have an answerphone may I leave a message?
                    Yes/No
If you are out, may I leave a message with a member of your family (if applicable)? Yes/No

Sometimes counselling appointments may become available at short notice. Please indicate if you would be happy to accept an appointment with very little notice

I can accept an appointment at short notice: Yes/No
I do not wish an appointment after all:

Your Name: ....please print)
Any comments: ....
....

Please note: Your name will not be placed on the waiting list unless this form is returned.

APPENDIX 7
Standard Paperwork

Please note these are sample letters; some services may use forms and some may be entering this information into the practice computer system

- Appointment Letter
- Acceptance for Counselling Letter
- DNA Letter
- Discharge Letter
- Letter not suitable for counselling
- Informed consent letter for copying of notes
- Client Attendance Record
- Client Summary Record

APPOINTMENT LETTER

Surgery Address

Patient Address

Date

Dear

Thank you for returning the opt-in form, indicating you would like a counselling appointment with me. I am sorry that you have had to wait until an appointment became available.

I am able to see you on:

....

at: .... Surgery.

If there is a problem with this time, could you please leave me a telephone message at the surgery (surgery phone no).

Yours sincerely

Your name
Practice Counsellor

ACCEPTED FOR COUNSELLING LETTER

Practice Address

PRIVATE & CONFIDENTIAL

Date:

Surgery Address

Dear Dr

Re:

Thank you for your referral of this patient to the Surgery Counselling Service.

Following an initial assessment, I am able to offer time limited primary care counselling to this client.

I will write to you again at the end of the counselling contract with an end of therapy summary report.

If you need any further information please contact me on the number below.

Yours sincerely

Your Name
Practice Counsellor

Your contact telephone number:

DNA LETTER

Surgery Address

Date

Client's Address

Dear

I am writing as I had expected to see you for a counselling appointment on ....
(day/date) at .... (time).

If you do wish to see me, for your next appointment on .... at
.... I would be grateful if you could
phone this number .... and leave me a
message to that effect.

If I do not hear from you by ....
(time and date), I will assume you do not wish to go
forward with the counselling at this time and will
inform your GP accordingly.

Yours sincerely

Your name
Practice Counsellor

DISCHARGE LETTER

Practice Address

Date

Surgery Address

Dear Dr ....

Re: Patient's name and date of birth

Thank you for referring .... to me for counselling. I saw him/her for "x" sessions ending on "date".

Paragraph summarising outcome of the counselling intervention. It is helpful to refer to any changes/improvements from the referral.

Any further recommendations.

Yours sincerely

Your name
Practice Counsellor

NOT SUITABLE FOR COUNSELLING LETTER

Name of Practice and Address

PRIVATE & CONFIDENTIAL

Date:

Surgery Address

Dear Dr

Re:

Thank you for your referral of this patient to the Surgery Counselling Service.

Following an initial assessment/*x* counselling sessions, regrettably our view is that this patient is not appropriate for the Surgery Counselling Service. Our service is able to see patients only for a time-limited counselling intervention of, on average, six sessions. The agreed referral protocols are for patients with mild to moderate mental health problems – please see our GP referral and information guidelines, copies of which are in all the surgeries or can be provided by our Team.

A short-term intervention, while initially seeming positive, may be damaging, as the time limit of the counselling will result in an ending before the work is in any way complete. This will mean the patient suffers another loss, and will have to start all over again in another service.

My recommendation is:

That this patient is referred for URGENT/non-urgent secondary mental health team assessment
Note:..

....

Or:

That longer term counselling could be of benefit to this patient. This may be offered through NHS referral to the Psychology Service, or local voluntary agencies such as .... that usually ask for a small financial contribution, or privately from the following sources:

- BACP: National directory of Counsellors & Psychotherapists: 0870-4435252
- UKCP: National directory of Counsellors & Psychotherapists: 020 7436 3002

For both the above directories we recommend that clients look for BACP Accredited or UKCP Registered Counsellors & Psychotherapists.

Yours sincerely

Your name
Practice Counsellor

INFORMED CONSENT LETTER FOR COPYING OF NOTES

Client's Address

Dear (counsellor)

In accordance with the Data Protection Act 1998, please send me copies of the notes taken when I attended for counselling sessions.

I acknowledge that once these notes are copied and sent in the post, you cease to be responsible for the confidentiality of the information contained therein. I also understand that should these notes be used as part of legal proceedings, they are likely to become public documents.

I enclose a cheque for £* as the administration fee for the release of these notes.

Please delete whichever does not apply:

I wish you to send the notes to my own address
I wish you to send the notes to my solicitor/ representative:

Name:
....
Address:..
....
Signed: ....
Name printed: ....
Date: ....

*Insert appropriate amount.

CLIENT ATTENDANCE RECORD

Client Attendance Record

Primary Care Counselling Service

GP Practice   Location

Referrer   Referral date:

Client reference no

Contracted number of sessions

Opt-in letter sent (date):   Opt-in received (date):

Session No.	Date	Attended	Cancelled	DNA
1				
2				
3				
4				
5				
6				
7				
8				
9				
10				
11				
12				
Totals				

CORE OM 1 Complete: CORE OM 2 Complete:

Discharge letter sent (date):

Counsellors Name ....

CLIENT SUMMARY RECORD

Page ..... of ......

Counsellor Name ....

Month/Year................................. Please Print

Please return a copy of this to the Co-ordinator on the last day of each month

Client ID	Referral Date	Referrer	Date Opt In Letter Sent	Date Opt In Received	Assessment Date	Counselling Start Date	Counselling End Date

INDEX